Crossway Bible Guide

Series editors: Ian Coffey (NT), Stephen Gaukroger (OT)
Old Testament editor: Stephen Dray

Dedicated to Mum and Dad, the best parents a son could have
and to the memory of Julie, the best sister a brother could have.
Thanks to Karen, Ann and Mary for typing the manuscript.
Thanks to Dr Tony Stuart and Mr Kingsley Dent for ideas and
suggestions during the writing of this book.

Psalms 1–72: Crossway Bible Guide

Alan Palmer

Crossway Books Leicester

CROSSWAY BOOKS
38 De Montfort Street, Leicester LE1 7GP, England

First published 1996

British Library Cataloguing in Publication Data

A catalogue record for this book is available from the British Library.

ISBN 1-85684-149-9

Set in Palatino

Typeset in Great Britain by Textype Typesetters, Cambridge

Printed in Great Britain by Clays Ltd., St Ives plc.

CONTENTS

Welcome!

These days, meeting together to study the Bible appears to be a booming leisure-time activity in many parts of the world. In the United Kingdom alone, it is estimated that over one million people each week meet in home Bible-study groups.

These Bible guides have been designed to help such groups and, in particular, those who lead them, but they are also eminently suitable for individual study. We are also aware of the needs of those who preach and teach to larger groups as well as the hard-pressed student, all of whom often look for a commentary that gives a concise summary and lively application of a particular passage.

We have therefore enlisted authors who are in the business of teaching the Bible to others and are doing it well. They have kept in their sights two clear aims:

1. To explain and apply the message of the Bible in non-technical language.
2. To encourage discussion, prayer and action on what the Bible teaches.

All of us engaged in the project believe that the Bible is the Word of God – given to us in order that people might discover him and his purposes for our lives. We believe that the sixty-six books which go to make up the Bible, although written by different people, in different places, at different times, through different circumstances, have a single unifying theme: That theme is Salvation. This means free forgiveness and the removal of all our guilt, it means the gift of eternal life and it means the wholeness of purpose and joy which God has designed us to experience here and now, all of this being made possible through the Lord Jesus Christ.

How to use your Crossway Bible Guide

These guides have been prepared both for personal study and for the leaders and members of small groups. More information about group study follows on the next few pages.

You can use this book very profitably as a personal study guide. The short studies are ideal for daily reading: the first of the following questions is usually aimed to help you with personal reflection (See *How to tackle personal Bible study*). If you prefer to settle down to a longer period of study you can use three to five studies at a time, and thus get a better overview of a longer Bible passage. In either case using the Bible Guide will help you to be disciplined about regular study, a habit that countless Christians have found greatly beneficial. (See also *How to tackle Psalms* for methods of selecting studies if you do not intend to use them all.)

Yet a third use for Crossway Bible Guides is as a quarry for ideas for the busy Bible teacher, providing outlines and application for those giving talks or sermons or teaching children. You will need more than this book can offer of course, but the way the Bible text is broken down, comments offered and questions raised may well suggest directions to follow.

How to tackle personal Bible study

We have already suggested that you might use this book as a personal study guide. Now for some more detail.

One of the best methods of Bible study is to read the text through carefully several times, possibly using different versions or translations. Having reflected on the material it is a good discipline to write down your own thoughts before doing anything else. At this stage the introduction of other books can be useful. If you are using this book as your main study resource, then read through the relevant sections carefully, turning up the Bible references that are mentioned. The questions at the end of each chapter are specifically designed to help you to apply the passage to your own situation. You may find it helpful to write your answers to the questions in your notes.

It is a good habit to conclude with prayer, bringing before God the things you have learned.

If this kind of in-depth study is too demanding for you and you have only a short time at your disposal, read the Bible passage, read the comments in the Bible Guide, think round one of the questions and commit what you have learned to God in a brief prayer. This would take about fifteen minutes without rushing it.

How to tackle your group Bible study

1. Getting help

If you are new to leading groups you will obviously want to get all the help you can from ministers and experienced friends. Books are also extremely helpful and we strongly recommend a book prepared by the series editors of the Crossway Bible Guides specifically for this series: *Housegroups: the leaders' survival guide*: edited by Ian Coffey and Stephen Gaukroger (Crossway Books). This book surveys the whole range of different types of group, asking what is the point of it all, what makes a good leader, how to tackle your meeting, how to help the members, how to study, pray, share, worship and plenty of other pointers, tips and guidelines.

This book is a 'must' for all leaders of small groups. It is written by a team of people widely experienced in this area. It is available at your local Christian bookshop. If you have difficulty in obtaining a copy write to Crossway Books, Norton Street, Nottingham, NG7 3HR, UK.

2. Planning your programme with a Crossway Bible Guide

This guide is a commentary on God's word, written to help a group to get the most out of their studies. Although it is never ideal to chop up Scripture into small pieces, which the authors never intended, huge chunks are indigestible and we have tried to provide a diet of bite-sized mouthfuls.

If you want to get an overview of the Bible book a in a series of meetings you will need to select appropriate studies for each meeting. Read them yourself first and prepare a short summary of the studies you are tackling for your group. Ideally you could write it on a sheet of A5 and hand a copy to each member.

Do not attempt to pack more than one study into one meeting but choose the crucial one which best crystallizes the message. There are examples in *How to tackle Psalms* below.

3. Resources

You will find any or all of these books of great value in providing background to your Bible knowledge. Put some of them on your Christmas list and build up your library.

> *New Bible Dictionary* or *New Concise Bible Dictionary* (IVP).
> *New Bible Atlas* (IVP).
> *New Bible Commentary (21st Century edition)* (IVP).
> *Everyday Life in Bible Times*: John Thompson (IVP).
> *The Bible User's Manual* (IVP).
> *The Lion Handbook to the Bible* (Lion Publishing).
> *The Message of the Bible* (Lion Publishing).
> *NIV Study Bible* (Hodder & Stoughton).
> *The Bible with pleasure*: Stephen Motyer (Crossway Books).

The relevant volume in the IVP Tyndale Commentary series will give you reliable and detailed help with any knotty points you may encounter.

4. Preparing to lead

Reading, discussing with friends, studying, praying, reflecting on life . . . preparation can be endless. But do not be daunted by that. If you wait to become the perfect leader you will never start at all. The really vital elements in preparation are:

▶ prayer (not only in words but an attitude of dependence on God, 'Lord, I can't manage this on my own')

▶ familiarity with the study passage (careful reading of the text, the Bible Guide study and any other resource books that throw light on it) and

▶ a clear idea of where you hope to get in the meeting (notes on your introduction, perhaps, recap what was covered at the last meeting, and what direction you hope the questions will take you in – don't force the group to give your answers).

Here is a short checklist for the busy group leader.

Have I prayed about the meeting?
Have I decided exactly what I want to achieve through the meeting?
Have I prepared the material?
Am I clear about the questions that will encourage positive group discussion?
Am I gently encouraging silent members?
Am I, again gently, quietening the chatterers?
Am I willing to admit ignorance?
Am I willing to listen to what the group says and to value their contributions?
Am I ready not to be dogmatic, not imposing my ideas on the group?
Have I planned how to involve the group in discovering for themselves?
Have I developed several 'prayer points' that will help focus the group?

Are we applying Scripture to our experience of real life or only using it as a peg to hang our opinions on?

Are we finding resources for action and change or just having a nice talk?

Are we all enjoying the experience together?

How to tackle Psalms

Now let's assume that you are planning an eight-week course of studies (you will have to make adjustments if you have more or fewer meetings). Where do you begin? This is entirely up to you and your groups of course, but to get you started, here are three possible routes you might take.

1. 'Top selection'

Some psalms are justly famous and if you have to miss out on the majority why not go for the best known and loved ones? Such as: Psalms 1, 8, 15, 19, 23, 42, 46, 67.

2. Pursue a theme

A favourite theme of the psalmists is how to turn sorrow, distress or confusion into praise. Although eight consecutive studies on this theme might appear to be in danger of repetition, you may find a wonderful variety. Here are some of them: Psalms 3, 4, 5, 6, 7, 13, 22, 38.

Use the contents list to pick out psalms on the theme of God's glory, joy, peace and so on.

3. Drawing close to God

Relating to God is a theme of most of the psalms and a concern for all Christians today. Here is a selection on that theme, but of course you can pick and choose: Psalms 15, 23, 26, 32, 37, 46, 51, 62.

These outlines are meant to be springboards for your own ideas, so please do not follow them slavishly. Adapt them for your own use, merge them or ignore them.

In any case many of the psalms will have to be left out of your studies, so why not begin or end your meeting by reading one or two other psalms as an aid to worship? This will give you a better flavour of the whole Book of Psalms, and remember, the psalms were meant to be sung, danced or wept not primarily studied.

What can we expect to learn from Psalms?

All Scripture is God-breathed and is useful (2 Timothy 3:16).
So how can the Psalms be 'useful' to us in our fellowship today?
The Psalms bring us into the nearer presence of God by:

▶ Showing us that our worship can legitimately include elements of the arts, i.e. music, poetry, drama and dance.

▶ Acting as a 'mirror for our souls', i.e. showing us what we are really like both as a church or fellowship and as individuals.

▶ Giving us words to express to God how we feel about him, his work and his creation. Also they help us more fully to express how we feel about everything that impacts our lives. They give us words of praise and when we need it words to seek God's pardon.

▶ Corporately and personally they can be used to renew our energy and resolve to live the life of faith.

Finding your way round this book

In our Bible Guides we have developed special symbols to make things easier to follow. Every study therefore has an opening section which is the passage in a nutshell.

The main section is the one that *makes sense of the passage*.

Questions

Every passage also has special questions for personal and group study after the main section. Some questions are addressed to us as individuals, some speak to us as members of our church or home group, while others concern us as members of God's people worldwide. The questions are deliberately designed:

- to get people thinking about the passage
- to apply the text to 'real life' situations
- to encourage reflection, discussion and action!

As a group leader you may well discover additional questions that will have special relevance to your group, so look out for these and note them in your preparation time.

Digging deeper

Some passages, however, require an extra amount of explanation, and we have put these into two categories. The first kind gives additional background material that helps us to understand something factual. For example, if we dig deeper into the gospels, it helps us to know who the Pharisees were, so that we can see more easily why they related to Jesus in the way they did. These background sections are marked with a spade.

Important doctrines

The second kind of explanatory section appears with passages which have important doctrines contained in them and which we need to study in more depth if we are to grow as Christians. Special sections that explain them to us in greater detail are marked with a face as above.

Welcome to the Psalms

Rave reviews!

Down the centuries the Psalms have fired the minds and imaginations of many Christians. Ambrose of Milan considered the Psalms the height of spirituality, viewing them as 'a kind of medicine for the salvation of the soul'. The German reformer Martin Luther thought them so important that he produced a 'New Testament and Psalms' version of the Bible, a practice followed by some publishers even today.

In the last century the great Baptist preacher C. H. Spurgeon spent over twenty years studying the Psalms. The result was his massive commentary, *The Treasury of David*. On completion of this monumental task he declared that he would never find a 'richer store house'.

In our own day enthusiasm for the Psalms has not diminished. Dr Billy Graham is so convinced about their benefits that he encourages all his listeners to read the Psalms regularly. He suggests that people follow his own practice of reading five psalms a day. In this way they can get through the entire collection in a month.

For many churches around the world the Psalms, either sung or read, are a vital aspect of their corporate worship. In a few churches they are the only musical contribution.

Why are the Psalms so popular?

Why are so many people attracted to the Psalms and what makes them so readable? There are three main reasons that contribute to their enduring popularity.

The Psalms reveal a God who has a heart for the arts

The Psalms are alive and attractive because they are so full of music. The title of the book of Psalms in the Greek version of the Old Testament (the Septuagint) is *psalmoi*. This originally indicated 'a striking or twitching of the fingers on a string'. It came to mean 'a sacred song accompanied by instruments'. The Psalms were written primarily to be sung, not read. Ronald Allen says that 'One can more easily separate dance from the dancer than Psalms from music. In music the Psalms come alive.'

There are many references to the use of instruments in the Psalms (e.g., Psalm 150). There are also musical instructions to be found in many of the titles (e.g., Psalm 22). While we do not know what all these instructions mean, this should not prevent us from putting our own music to these ancient songs. It would be wrong to miss the significance of the fact that the longest book in the Bible is a book of music. Martin Luther wrote, 'He who despises music does not please me. Music is a gift of God, not a gift of men. After theology I accord to music the highest place and the highest honour.'

The title of the book of Psalms in the Hebrew Bible is *tehillim*. This simply means 'Praises'. Robert Weber writes, 'Here is the heart of praise for the Old Testament people of God'. If this is the case then 'music' must be considered as a vital ingredient to praise and worship. It seems that when the Holy Spirit is at work among the people of God it is not long before there is a new song on their lips (Ephesians 5:18–20).

The Psalms reveal a God with a passion for poetry

One quarter of the Old Testament is in poetic form. The Psalms are simply poetry set to music. The most reasonable explanation for this is that poetry is the best medium with which to communicate our feelings. For, as Laurence Perrine writes, poetry is 'a kind of language that says more and says it more intensively than does ordinary language'. Here we find words to express how we really feel to God.

When we call the Psalms 'poetry' we should be aware that Hebrew poetry is quite different from the rhyming variety that we may be familiar with. Professor Alan Harmon reminds us that the Psalms have to 'be read as a Middle Eastern book of poetry translated into English'.

Its poetic form is based around a literary structure known as 'parallelism'. This is where the same idea is described in different ways to give a fuller sense of meaning. There are various different types of parallelism to be found in the Psalms.

Sometimes the first line of a pair is echoed in the second.

O LORD, how many are my foes!
  How many rise up against me! (Psalm 3:1)

Sometimes the second line develops the first line a bit further, often adding ideas or elements to the original thought:

Come let us bow down in worship,
  let us kneel before the LORD our Maker. (Psalm 95:6)

In some cases the second line begins with 'but', and presents the opposite of the first line:

For evil men will be cut off,
  But those who hope in the LORD will inherit the land. (Psalm 37:9)

In other cases the first line is explained by the second, often with figures of speech or word pictures:

Your tongue plots destruction;
  it is like a sharpened razor,
  you who practise deceit. (Psalm 52:2)

Students of the Psalms believe that it is possible to divide them up into different 'categories' or 'types'. Whether a particular psalm fits in these categories is determined by content and literary structure. While it is not possible for every psalm to be categorized in this way, certain 'types' of psalms are recognizable.

Five of the main types of Psalms are:

- a hymn of praise (e.g., Psalms 8, 19, 33, 103, 145–150)

- a song of thanksgiving (e.g., Psalms 18, 21, 92, 138)

- a lament by an individual or community (e.g., Psalms 3, 5, 13, 17, 22, 31, 44, 80, 126, 137)

- a song of trust and meditation (e.g., Psalms 11, 16, 23, 91, 121, 131)

- a wisdom psalm (e.g., Psalms 37, 49, 73, 112, 128, 133).

The Psalms reveal a God who has provided psalms for all seasons

In the middle of the Bible God has provided what Saint Augustine called 'a looking glass of the soul'. Here we can see ourselves and our situations. There is nothing we can experience which is not reflected in the writings of the psalmist. John Calvin recognized this when he called the book of Psalms the 'anatomy of the soul'. He went on to say that 'there is not an emotion of which anyone can be conscious that is not here represented as in a mirror'.

The Psalms not only reflect what is going on in our lives, they also give us the words to express to God how we feel about it. Saint Athanasius wrote, 'Most of Scripture speaks to us while the Psalms speak for us'. Here we can find appropriate words to tell the Lord exactly what is going on in our lives. The Psalms are not only songs for us to sing, they can also become prayers that we can pray.

Who wrote the Psalms?

We know that King David was a gifted composer and musician (see 2 Samuel 23:1). It is hardly surprising then to find that nearly half of the songs in the book of Psalms are attributed to him, seventy-three in all. But he is not the only author who contributed to this marvellous collection.

Familiar characters like King Solomon (Psalms 72 and 127)

and Moses (Psalm 90) make their contribution. Other writers may be less well known to us. A man named Asaph has twelve psalms attributed to him (Psalms 50, 73–83). Two psalms are by Heman and Ethan, the Ezrahites (Psalms 88 and 89). A further twelve psalm are written by a family group known as 'The sons of Korah' (Psalms 42–49, 84–85 and 87–88). There are also 'anonymous psalms' whose writers remain unknown to us (Psalms 1, 2, 33, 66, 111–121 *etc.*). However, because David wrote the majority of the psalms the collection is most often linked to his name. That is why we refer to them as 'The Psalms of David'.

When were the Psalms written?

Half the psalms were written by David in the tenth century BC. Some were written much earlier than this and some much later. Psalm 90 is the earliest we can date and it comes from Moses in the fifteenth century BC. One of the latest, Psalm 137, was written by a Jewish exile who had returned to Jerusalem from Babylon in the late fifth century BC. This means that the Psalms we have today were written over a thousand year period.

How are the Psalms put together?

The Psalter (the technical name for the collection of psalms) contains five Books of Psalms. It is modelled on the 'Pentateuch' (the five books of Moses, i.e., Genesis to Deuteronomy). Orthodox Jewish teaching is that Moses gave Israel the five books of the Law. King David's gift was the five books of poetry known as the Psalms. The books are as follows:

Book 1	Psalms 1–41
Book 2	Psalms 42–72
Book 3	Psalms 73–89
Book 4	Psalms 90–106
Book 5	Psalms 107–150

Titles and technical terms

The titles or superscriptions which we find at the top of many of the psalms were probably added a long time after the original song was written. Possibly these additions were made by an editor when the psalms were being put together into a collection. They usually contain either some musical instruction or give some historical background to the psalm. Some psalms have no titles.

Cursing psalms

There are a number of psalms which contain a strong element of seeming vindictiveness, hatred or cursing. These have caused real problems to Christians and non-Christians alike. The best way to deal with these psalms, especially in the light of the New Testament, is not to ignore them but to seek to understand and face their concerns squarely. Here are some of the factors to consider:

1. They have been included in the Bible. This means that we must take them seriously (see 2 Timothy 3:16).
2. They are spoken in the context of faith, believing God alone should execute vengeance.
3. The psalmist thinks of his enemies as God's enemies, who, as such, are to be hated.
4. David was in no way a vindictive man.
5. The New Testament actually emphasizes the reality of judgment on all evil doers.
6. Christians may not wish to take and use these cries for themselves but may prefer to 'translate them into affirmations of God's judgment and into denunciations of the "spiritual hosts of wickedness" which are the real enemy' (Derek Kidner, Vol. I, *Psalms* 1–77 (IVP, 1973), p. 32).

Above all we need to remind ourselves that the Psalms are 'the windows of the soul'. They are an honest expression of what the psalmist was really thinking at the time. The truth is that none of us have been completely free of such thoughts. This is probably why we find these 'cursing psalms' so uncomfortable to read. The psalmists' total openness can be very threatening indeed! It is comforting to know that J. I. Packer's words remain true for all of us, 'God knows the absolute worst about us and yet still loves us'.

Examples of cursing psalms include: Psalms 7, 35, 58, 59, 69, 109, 137, 139. Some psalms contain a smaller element: Psalms 5:10; 17:13; 40:14; 55:9; 104:35; 129:5.

How did the ancient people of God use the Psalms?

Although they were written by individuals the Psalms came to play a vital role in the spiritual life of the whole community of Israel. They were 'Israel's hymnbook' and were used extensively in the context of corporate worship.

Psalms were sung by pilgrims as they made their way up to Jerusalem to worship at the temple. These are known as the 'Songs of the Ascents' (Psalms 120–134). The temple choirs used them as dramatic 'sung requests' to gain entry to the place of worship (Psalm 24). The congregation used them to express their worship to God for his greatness, forgiveness, love and mercy (Psalms 8, 22, 48, 51, 65, 103). When it came to a time of praise the Psalms were much in evidence (Psalms 145–150). The Psalms were very much part of the very fabric of Jewish worship. They still are today.

How are the Psalms used in the New Testament?

When we turn to the New Testament we discover that the Psalms figure significantly. The Lord Jesus himself sang the Psalms all his life. When he came to Jerusalem with his parents for the Feast of Passover he would have sung the Songs of Ascent (Psalms 120–134). In celebrating the Passover each year he would have sung the Hallel Psalms (Psalms 113–118, 136).

Those who wrote the history of his life saw in the Psalms references to him. For instance:

▶ When Jesus entered Jerusalem the crowds greeted him with words taken directly from the Psalms (Luke 19:38 and Psalm 118:26).

▶ In his debates with the authorities Jesus referred to their rejection of him by appealing to the Psalms (Luke 20:17–18 and Psalm 118:22).

▶ In a discussion of who he really was, again Jesus pointed people back to the Psalms (Luke 20:42–43 and Psalm 110:1).

The Lord Jesus took part in singing some of the Psalms at the Last Supper (Matthew 26:30).

▶ When he was facing the most awful suffering on the cross he cried out using words taken from Israel's ancient hymn book (Matthew 27:46; Mark 15:34 and Psalm 22:1).

▶ The words of the priests who threw abuse at him, while he hung on the cross, seem to be echoes of sentiments expressed in the Psalms (Matthew 27:39–44; Mark 15:31–32; Luke 23:35 and Psalm 22:7–8).

▶ The fact that the soldiers left his garment undivided was seen as a fulfilment of what was written by the psalmist (John 19:23–24 and Psalm 22:18).

▶ The gruesome physical effects of crucifixion are apparently predicted in Psalm 22:14–17.

▶ Even the Lord Jesus' last words on the cross, 'into your hands I commit my spirit' were taken directly from Psalm 31:5 (Luke 23:46).

Following the resurrection Jesus managed to convince two discouraged disciples that he was the Messiah by referring back to the Old Testament Scriptures. He showed them how all these writings were pointing forward to him and his mission and ministry. There is little doubt that the Psalms were a part of this Bible study that Jesus conducted. This guided tour of the Old Testament led to these two disciples experiencing a new revelation of Christ and what someone has called 'spiritual heart-burn' (Luke 24:32). Later Jesus told all the gathered disciples that the Psalms were a major part of his teaching programme while he was with them (Luke 24:44). It is no wonder that all the early writers of the New Testament felt that the Psalms were so important in their understanding of who Jesus was and what he had come to do.

Ronald Allen says that the New Testament is 'awash with the Psalms'. There are approximately 360 quotations from the Hebrew Bible in the New Testament and nearly one-third (112) of these are from the Psalms.

The early Christians turned to the Psalms and saw Jesus pictured there. They also turned to the Psalms to find texts to preach on concerning the resurrection (Acts 2:25–28; 29–35; Psalm 16:8–11; Psalm 110:1). In times of testing and persecution they looked for comfort and encouragement there as well (Acts 4:23–26 and Psalm 2:1–2).

How should we read the Psalms for ourselves?

As we read these wonderful songs we can learn more about what pleases God. We can identify with the experiences of those who wrote them. We can grow in our devotion to the Lord. If we have been flagging spiritually we may even find that they give us a new enthusiasm for the life of Faith. The words of Saint Augustine are a fitting summary. He said that the Psalms 'kindled his love for God, (and) they breathed fresh life into his spiritual pilgrimage.'

Psalm 1

The doorway to the Psalms

A choice is presented to us. We can choose the path that leads to life or the path that leads to death.

The book of Psalms has been compared to a mansion with 150 rooms. In each room we can make new discoveries about God and about ourselves. Psalm 1 is the doorway through which we enter this large and exciting building.

The first psalm is not only the entry point to the book, it also sets the style for what follows. All that follows should be read in the light of Psalm 1. For here we have set before us God's perception of the true state of every man and woman. The Creator speaks in clear and uncomplicated terms to his creatures. There are only two options for us while living here on earth. Either we are for God or we are against him. This theme can be traced through the book of Psalms and right through the entire Bible.

Ultimate destinies

We are introduced immediately to the present and ultimate destinies of humankind. The first and last words of the psalm (verses 1 and 6) indicate the stark alternatives. The psalm begins with a blessing and ends with a calamity: the alternative destinies are set before us and we must consider our choices very carefully. One way will lead to life and one to death (see Deuteronomy 30:15–18).

The psalmist (the author remains anonymous) starts the song with a description of a person who lives a life approved by God. They are known as the 'blessed ones'. Jesus begins his teaching in the Sermon on the Mount in a similar way and for similar reasons (see Matthew 5:1–11). Both Jesus and the psalmist want to begin with a clear definition of a life that pleases God, everything else flows from this.

The godly life

Those who live a life blessed by God are described by using first negative terms and then positive. They are applauded for what they do not do before they are commended for what they do. Those the Lord approves of do not shape their lives by taking the advice of people who have no regard for him. They do not constantly associate with people who persistently do the wrong thing. As John Stott points out '. . . still less do they remain permanently among the cynical who openly scoff at God' (verse 1). The words 'walk', 'stand' and 'sit' are meant to indicate a steady downward progression which the godly must avoid at all costs.

Now the psalmist moves from the negative to the positive. He shows what a godly life looks like (verse 2). Firstly, the man or woman of God loves his Word. Here it is called the 'law of the LORD'. This refers not just to the Ten Commandments, or even to the rules and regulations given by Moses, but to all God-given instruction on how life should be lived. The 'law of the LORD' and the 'Word of God' are virtually equivalent because both reveal what God is like and how he wants us to conduct ourselves.

To gain the optimum benefits from God's word or law we have to give time to absorbing it. The psalmist speaks of 'meditating' upon it day and night (verse 2). The word 'meditate' suggests 'constantly chewing over the Word of God until we can digest all the good things it contains'.

Godly people do not listen to the wicked but constantly depend upon the wisdom of God. They are described as being like a well-rooted tree (verse 3). This is a picture that occurs several times in the Bible (Jeremiah 17:7–8; Psalm 92:12; Isaiah 44:4). These people are able to draw upon refreshing streams or irrigation channels. Perhaps the inner resources given by the Holy Spirit may be implied here (see John 7:37–39). Because they are constantly being refreshed they are continually fruitful. We know from the teaching of Jesus that bearing fruit is one of the evidences that we are in a living connection to the 'true vine' (John 15:1–8). Another result of this continual refreshment is that when things heat up the godly person does not wither. The life that is rooted in the Lord is bound to prosper, perhaps not in material ways but in things that really count.

The ungodly life

After this wonderful picture of a person who is both a delight to God and delighted in God, the next description brings us up with quite a jolt. The contrast is almost overwhelming (verses 4–6). The first two words of verse 4, 'not so', tell us that none of the good things attributed to the godly apply to the wicked. They have made their choice to live a life without reference to God. Indeed, it is more serious than that. The wicked are those who actively and intentionally do not believe in God. They are described as the worthless by-products of the threshing process. They are of no more substance than the husks or chaff that get blown away by the wind (verse 4). Those who refuse to turn to God and accept his forgiveness will, in the final analysis, lose everything (verse 5). They will not be able to stand up under his scrutiny and, when judgment is passed, they will be pronounced guilty (verse 5).

In case we have missed the contrasting results of our choices for or against God, the psalmist brings them home to us again in the final verse (verse 6). While God observes the godly with joy in his heart, his observation of the wicked causes him pain. He knows that if they fail to turn to him in the end he will have to turn away from them and this will result in their destruction.

Questions

1. The psalmist discourages us from spending too much time with those who have no time for God (verse 1). What particular relationships, if any, do you think Christians should avoid? How does this affect our attitude towards evangelism?
2. Dr Billy Graham has gone on record as saying that if he had his time over again he would spend more time studying God's Word. Why is it so important for Christians to take time to study the Bible?
3. The psalm states quite clearly that the wicked will perish (verse 6). If we really believe this how will it affect the way we set priorities in our church life?

Chaff

The wicked are described in verse 4 as 'chaff' which gets blown away by the wind. This picture is a common one in the Bible (Psalm 35:5; Isaiah 17:13; Luke 3:16–17). It is taken from a farming practice. There were no combine harvesters so the corn had to be cut by hand and the husks separated from the grain by a process called 'threshing'. A threshing floor was used, usually a hard, flat surface on the side of a hill, well exposed to the wind. The wheat was lifted by a large winnowing fan or shovel and thrown into the air so that the grain would drop down and be collected, while the light husks of the chaff would be blown away by the wind.

Psalm 2

World in rebellion

Society has a choice to make. It can either humbly accept God's Lordship or live in rebellion against him.

If Psalm 1 describes choices and their conse-quences for the individual, then Psalm 2 does the same task for society as a whole.

Although this psalm has no title, it is thought to be the work of King David. The New Testament writers certainly believed this to be the case (Acts 4:25 and 13:33–4). It may have been written as a song to celebrate his coronation. The language indicates, however, that this was not a time of undisturbed joy for King David. International storm clouds seem to have been gathering on the horizon (verses 1–3). Apparently some of the subject peoples were plotting to overthrow the monarchy!

Rebellion on a grand scale

Looking a little deeper we can see that there is a much bigger picture here than mere political intrigue. This psalm speaks about rebellion on a vastly grander scale! With hindsight we can imme-diately see the universal application here. Put in this context the plotting is not against a human king but a heavenly one (verse 2).

Ever since Adam and Eve declared their independence from God by choosing to ignore his advice, humankind has been in

33

rebellion against the Great King of Heaven (Genesis 3:1–24). Every unconverted person has a natural inclination to say 'No' to God. This deep-seated rebellion surfaced in people's reaction to Jesus and their ultimate plot to try to silence him for ever on the cross.

People do not want to be shackled by what they consider to be religious rules and regulations (verse 3). They 'plot' or murmur against the constraints religion might put on their freedom. The natural inclination of people who do not know God is to resist his rule. All this rebelliousness leads nowhere, says the psalmist; it's all in vain (verse 1).

A psalm for the persecuted

This psalm has always come to prominence when the people of God are under the pressure of persecution. When society is rejecting the Lord it is not usually very long before they begin to reject his people. The early church recognized this and turned to this psalm for confirmation and comfort (Acts 4:25).

The early church looked to heaven for help (Acts 4:29–31). The psalmist does the same. He lifts his eyes from the confusion on earth to find clarification from heaven. He is encouraged to find that God is still in control. He sits in the control room of the universe (verse 4). The rebellious nations will be rebuked like naughty children. These rebels will shake with fear when the mighty king reveals his anger (verse 5).

Here there is even more encouragement for God's persecuted people. He promises to get involved with world affairs at a personal level. The Lord has appointed his person to rule. Originally this spoke of David but it points beyond him to King Jesus (verse 6).

The King is described as God's Son (verse 7). We know that both David and Solomon were called 'the son of God' (Psalm 89:27; 2 Samuel 7:14). But someone greater than David or Solomon is pictured here. The New Testament recognized that this title properly belongs to Jesus (John 1:49; Matthew 26:63; Mark 14:61). The book of Revelation tells us that what we read here will eventually be true. Jesus will rule over the nations of the earth (Revelation 19:16). He will rule with strength and rigour (verse 9, see also Revelation 2:27; 12:5; 19:15).

The psalmist now offers some sound advice to rebels of every generation (verses 10–12). The best way to approach God is with a respectful servant spirit. This will lead to joy not slavery (verse 11). Servants of the King will offer him homage, willing and full hearted obedience (verse 12). They will recognize that he has a right to be angry because of their rebellion. However, he is willing to receive them graciously if they seek to find refuge in him (verse 12).

Questions

1. What things cause you to resist God's Lordship in your life?
2. In what ways can your local church serve the locality and so serve the King?
3. What will society look like when the Lord Jesus is in control? What implications should Jesus' Kingship have for us today?

Anointing

To 'anoint' with oil was a common practice in biblical times (Ruth 3:3, 'pefume' NIV). It was a token of respect shown to a welcome guest and failure to carry this out was seen as a lack of hospitality (Luke 7:46). People and things were anointed to signify that they were 'set apart' for a special God-given task. For example, Jacob anointed the stone he used as a 'pillow' on which to rest his head (Genesis 28:18). Prophets (1 Kings 19:16), priests (Leviticus 4:3) and kings (1 Samuel 10:1), were all anointed. David was anointed three times, first in anticipation of his kingship (1 Samuel 16:13), then as king over Judah (2 Samuel 2:4), then as king over all Israel (2 Samuel 5:3).

The phrase 'The LORD's anointed' was used to describe the king who was God's special choice (1 Samuel 12:3; Lamentations 4:20). The term 'Anointed One', from which we get the word 'Messiah', is used in verse 2 of this psalm to refer to David. Christians believe that this phrase ultimately refers to the Lord Jesus (see Daniel 9:25 and Acts 4:26). He combines within his own person the three anointed offices of Prophet, Priest and King.

Psalm 3

Confidence in time of trouble

We can turn to God for help in a family crisis.

This is the first psalm with a title or super-scription. These were not part of the original texts but were added by editors much later. The information they give often helps the reader to appreciate more fully the contents of the psalm (see p. 25).

According to the title this psalm was written by David and is one of the fourteen psalms which are linked with particular historical episodes in his life (Psalms 3, 7, 18, 30, 34, 51, 52, 54, 56, 57, 59, 60, 63 and 142).

A family in turmoil

It was composed at a time when David's family was in turmoil (for the background to this psalm see 2 Samuel 15). Godly parents are not immune from the anguish of family trauma! David was a parent in pain. His son Absalom was plotting to overthrow him (2 Samuel 15:1–13). It is not difficult to imagine the anguish this must have caused him. If he attempted to put down the rebellion it might entail the death of his own son. If he did nothing his kingdom might well be snatched from him. It was a terrible dilemma! History records that David chose the nonconfrontational option. At face value he left Jerusalem to avoid bloodshed. The real reason may well have been to prevent a possible encounter with Absalom (2 Samuel 15:14).

To add insult to injury David had to make his exodus from the capital city under a shower of abuse (2 Samuel 16:5–8). Here we have a father who has been cut to the heart by his son's actions and stung in his spirit by a hail of accusations (2 Samuel 16:10–11). It is little wonder that the song he writes begins with a passionate cry to God (verse 3).

David begins the psalm with a prayer. It is not the kind of praying where we ask God for something but more a matter of telling him exactly how we feel. He was not only being overwhelmed by the sheer numbers of his enemies (verse 1), he was also facing an attempt to undermine his confidence in God (verse 2, see also 2 Samuel 16:8).

Growing in confidence

The psalmist resolves not to be crushed by his circumstances, however terrible. He speaks his faith out loud in the presence of God and in this way reassures himself (verse 3). Sometimes simply saying out loud what we really believe about God helps! He recognizes that God is his shield (verse 3, see also Genesis 15:1; Deuteronomy 33:29). The Hebrew language has a play on words here. The word translated 'shield' can also be rendered 'Sovereign Lord'. In this way God's character and his offer of protection are inseparably linked!

This psalm speaks of God as our protector and also helps us to see him as our encourager. He is the one who 'lifts up our heads' (verse 3). Here is the picture of a person lying prostrate before a great king, seeking his mercy and help. The monarch literally lifts the supplicant by the chin, in this way symbolizing that his help is assured. David was 'lifted out' of his discouragement by God.

The psalm now traces his growing confidence. He is sure that God will answer his prayers. The word 'hill' (verse 4) indicates the city of Jerusalem, the earthly symbol of God's presence and power. It is God, and not Absalom, who will determine David's future (see Acts 2:34–35). Reassured by this he can now get a good night's sleep (verse 5). He is no longer prone to panic attacks, even when the odds are stacked against him. Like many people through history David had discovered the truth of the saying that 'one with God is a majority'.

The last two verses of the psalm demonstrate how far David has come in his journey from fear to faith. He is confidently asking God to act on his behalf (verse 7). He rests in the assurance that God can easily take the 'bite' out of his enemies' wicked schemes! He concludes his song with a statement of faith and a prayer for others who need a blessing from the Lord (verse 8).

Questions

1. To what lengths are we prepared to go to avoid confrontation? Why do we try so hard to avoid confrontation?
2. Opposition and trouble can sometimes undermine our confidence in God and make us 'run away' from the problem. What lesson can we learn from the experiences of Elijah (see 1 Kings 19), Jonah (see Jonah 1–4) and Peter (see Luke 22)?
3. Do our churches have a strategy in place to help 'parents in pain'. If not how could we go about establishing one?
4. Why is society at large such a difficult place to raise a family?

Directions for the worship leader

The title contains the word 'psalm'. This is the Hebrew word *mizmor*. It is thought that this indicated that this song was to have musical accompaniment.

The word *Selah* occurs three times in this psalm (verses 2, 4 and 8) and appears seventy-one times in the book of Psalms. It can also be found three times in the prophecy of Habakkuk (3:3, 9, 13). We are not sure of its exact meaning. Several suggestions have been made. It could be connected with the word *salal*, 'to lift up', an instruction for more instruments to be included and to 'raise' the volume. Or it could be derived from the word *shalah* 'to rest'. In this case it may have been used to signify a quieter time to reflect upon what has been said. Or as someone has suggested, although not very seriously, it could have been the word David used when he broke a string on his harp! Probably the best approach is to take *selah* as indicating a musical interlude to pause and reflect on what has just been said, a breathing space for us to absorb what God is trying to say to us at that particular point in the psalm.

Psalm 4

Let me rest in your peace Lord

When exhausted by emotional turmoil, in our weakness we should turn to the Lord.

There is a strong link between this and the previous psalm. Indeed, both psalms were probably written against the background of Absalom's rebellion (see 2 Samuel 15).

David had coped well with the dreadful issues of the day. As night fell, however, the strain of his family circumstances and the state of his nation began to take its toll. He writes a response to express his feelings and thoughts at the end of a trying day.

Dealing with discouragement

As he feels the dark shadow of discouragement creeping up on him he turns to God in prayer (verse 1), approaching him with inner confidence that he can always be trusted to do the right thing. He asks to be granted relief from his distress. Literally he asks God to get him out of the 'tight corner' he finds himself in.

From prayer David turns to the subject of problem people (verse 2). He asks them a very direct question. How long will they continue to spread lies about him? He recognizes that there is a direct link between the kind of god people believe in and the kind of life they lead. If they follow false gods it is not long before they begin to deal in falsehood (verse 2). We may not worship idols but it is possible for us to have less than a biblical view of the character of God. If we have a defective understanding of God there are bound to be defective areas of our lives. However, if we get the right view of God our lives will reflect this. Charles Swindoll rightly observes that 'the closer you get to the authentic, the less you care about the artificial'.

When we are in a real relationship with the true and living God we soon recognize how special this friendship is (verse 3). David knew that an important aspect of being 'set apart' for God was spending quality time with him. Interestingly, before Jesus sent his disciples out on a preaching tour he asked them to spend time with him (see Mark 3:13–14).

Dealing with anger

The psalmist moves on from our relationship to God to look at our responses to other people (verses 4–5). He recognizes that it is very easy to become angry, especially with those who are unkind or unloving to us. David had good reason to be angry with Absalom and others who were trying to make his life a misery. He realized that to explode was not the appropriate response for the godly person to make. Yet storing up anger can be very destructive to ourselves and others. The psychiatrist Dr Lewis McBurney writes,

> We need to realize that anger is part of our humanness. It is not necessarily destructive, but bottled up is like a time bomb waiting to go off . . . The sin is not being angry but nursing anger – keeping it bottled up within, which most of us do. Most of us let anger fester and boil until it becomes rage and hostility. Or we contain it so tightly that it turns into frustration and depression. Since most of us don't go round killing one another, we tend to express our anger in depression. (*Leadership Magazine*, Spring Quarter, 1991)

Instead when we are angry (literally 'trembling with rage'), we are to take a 'cooling off' period. David's advice is that we 'sleep on it' and give the issue further consideration. If we react too quickly we are bound to end up doing the sinful, rather than the sensible, thing (Ephesians 4:26). Instead of 'hot anger' we need to demonstrate humble trust in the Lord.

To add to David's difficulties he had some friends around him who were in the depths of depression (verse 6). To these people he gives a word of personal testimony (verse 7). He tells them that when he places his trust in God, God fills him with a joy that is unaffected by external circumstances. Verse 7 draws on the imagery of harvest. Palestinian peasants reaped two separate harvests each year, the grain harvest and the grape harvest. The 'new wine' was made from the first juice extracted from the grapes and could be very intoxicating. Despite the stresses and strains he faced, David was 'intoxicated' with joy in the Lord he trusted.

In the last part of this psalm he is again at peace. He has been able to give his problems to the Lord and now can look forward to a restful night's sleep.

Questions

1. J. C. Massee said, 'If you are going to be a man or woman of God, it is mandatory that you spend a great deal of time alone'. Why is it so important to spend time alone with God?
2. 'Trust in the LORD' (verse 5). Why are trust and worry mutually exclusive?
3. In your local church, when people separate from each other because of anger, how are they brought together again?
4. Why is it so natural for humans to create 'false gods' for themselves (Psalm 4:2)?

More advice for the worship leader

The title in the NIV is 'to the director of music'. Whoever had to make the choice of musical accompaniment believed that this psalm should be sung to music played on stringed instruments. The Hebrew word used for stringed instruments is *Niginoth*. It could refer to a variety of stringed instruments available in those days. There was a basic form of harp known as the *kinnor*. This appears to have come in various forms and with different numbers of strings available. Or the word could refer to any instruments that were played with the hand, such as, harps and cymbals. C. H. Spurgeon comments on this phrase: 'The joy of the Jewish church was so great that they needed music to set forth the delightful feelings of their souls'.

Psalm 5

God of mercy

 David's enemies are at work again mounting another sustained campaign of slander against him. As was his usual practice in these circumstances David turns to God in prayer. He begins the psalm with a prayer that is made up of almost as many sighs as words (verse 1). There are times in our lives when only the Spirit can interpret what we really want to say to God (Romans 8:26–27). Commenting on these verses C. H. Spurgeon wrote that 'groanings which cannot be uttered are often the prayers which cannot be refused'. David knew something of this experience.

Sacrificial praying

The psalmist begins to find the appropriate words to explain to God exactly what he wants from him. He needs to enlist the help of One who is both his Sovereign (King) and his Saviour (God) (verse 2). He is both persistent and expectant in making his requests known to God (verse 3). The language of verse 3 suggests that David saw his prayer life as part of his on-going

43

sacrificial living for God (Romans 12:1–3). The word 'wait' (verse 3) speaks of eagerly awaiting God's answer to prayer. The prophets use it in a similar way (Isaiah 21:6–8; Micah 7:7; Habakkuk 2:1).

As David spends time in God's presence he becomes increasingly aware of just how holy he is (verse 4). He is not able to tolerate evil in any form (verse 4). The psalmist logically concludes from this that people who are evil have no place in the presence of a Holy God (verse 5, see also Deuteronomy 32:21–22). Those who hurt people with their words or weapons will find no support in heaven (verse 6).

Not one of us is without sin (1 John 1:8, 10). David recognizes this and knows that he is in as much need of mercy as the next person (verse 6). It is on the basis of God's mercy, and not his own merit, that David is able to approach him. The psalmist recognizes that the only posture available to a sinner in the presence of a Holy God is flat on the floor. To 'bow down' is to prostrate one's self (verse 7).

Life is never easy

David knew very well that living a godly life was never easy. It has always involved treading difficult paths. This is why we have to seek God's guidance to help us navigate the tricky routes (verse 8). Not only do we have to negotiate difficult paths, we also meet difficult people along the way. We will undoubtedly encounter people similar to those described by David here whose words are both deceitful and deadly (verse 9). In the end, however, they will get caught out by their own crafty plans (verse 10).

The psalm now concludes on a positive note. David affirms in the presence of God that those who seek him find not only protection but joy (verses 11–12).

Questions

---

1. How can we ensure we really depend on the Spirit in prayer?

2. Have we lost the sense of 'awe' in the presence of God? How can we recover it?
3. What picture does the word 'holy' conjure up in your mind? What does this psalm tell us about God's holiness?

Biblical puns

In verse 9 David's enemies are described as having 'throats that are (like) open graves'. In the Hebrew language of the Old Testament there is a pun here. The word 'grave' sounds similar to the word 'heart'. Jesus picked up on this, recognizing that every form of evil found its origins in the deepest recesses of the human heart (Jeremiah 5:16; Romans 3:13; Mark 7:20–23).

Psalm 6

Be gentle with me Lord

When we know that we have displeased the Lord, we should want to put things right.

We discover David feeling somewhat 'fragile' in this psalm. He knows that he has done something which has grieved and displeased God. He also realizes that he deserves to be punished, but he asks God to deal with him in mercy rather than in anger (verses 1–2).

Badly shaken

David is in a bad way. Whatever has gone on in the lead-up to writing this song has shaken him badly (verse 2). His whole person is in trauma ('bones' here refers to the whole man, verse 2). Physically, emotionally and spiritually David is in a desperate state (verses 2–3), so much so that he fears for his life (verse 5).

In this terrible situation he turns to God for help. He appeals to him on the grounds of his covenant love. This kind of love is expressed in God's eternal commitment to us. God's guarantee of this 'unfailing love' is his own character (verse 4). He cannot stop loving us because he has made a promise not to do so.

There is a note of urgency about David's prayer (verse 5). If God does not intervene death may well silence his songs of praise.

The Psalms are always refreshingly honest about how life really is. David was experiencing the kind of exhaustion that comes from extended periods of emotional stress. He felt the pain of the situation at the very centre of his being. His feelings about the matter could only be expressed in 'groans' and 'tears' (verses 6–7).

Whatever his enemies had done to him had brought the king to a very low ebb indeed.

God hears

It seems that between verses 7 and 8 something very positive has happened to bring about a change in David's demeanour. Perhaps God had met with him in some special way, or perhaps the situation which was troubling him had been resolved. We do not know for sure. What can be said for certain is that he has moved out of depression and into a state of mind where he is able to declare the faithfulness of God: God has heard his prayers. He now confidently proclaims that his enemies' taunts were groundless. Those who wanted to hurt David were saying that God would never answer his prayers (verse 9 implied). This has been proved false and those who made such a foolish statement deserved to blush with embarrassment (verse 10).

Questions

1. What can we do when we know that all is not right in our relationship with God?
2. How can churches encourage real repentance in the lives of believers? (Note that repentance is 'a change of mind followed by a change of heart, followed by a change in direction. It is a radical turning away from sin.)
3. 'How long, O LORD?' (verse 3). Why does God sometimes 'keep us waiting' for deliverance? How can we use these waiting times constructively?

The worship band

The title gives instructions for this psalm to be accompanied by stringed instruments. It may be that these were 'eight stringed' instruments. The word *sheminith* can be translated 'eighth'. Some scholars believe that what we have here is an instruction to play in the 'tenor' or 'bass' range. Instruments that played in these ranges may have been considered most suitable to accompany a song of this serious nature. We can only guess at this.

Sheol

The experts are not sure as to the origin of this word (verse 5, NIV note). It may come from the verb meaning 'to demand'. This would reflect the idea that death is always taking new victims: it is 'never satisfied' (Proverbs 27:20). Or it could come from the verb meaning 'to hollow'. This gives the idea of *Sheol* being a very large 'area' or 'space' to which human souls go after death. *Sheol* is used in various ways in the Old Testament. It is sometimes used to refer to 'death' or 'the grave' as here (see Isaiah 38:10; 1 Kings 2:6). On other occasions it refers to the state to which all men go after death. John Blanchard writes, 'Everyone goes there, from the best to the worst. There is no mention of pleasure for the righteous or punishment for the unrighteous' (*Whatever happened to Hell?* (Evangelical Press, 1993)).

It is described as a place of 'shadows', 'darkness' and 'silence' (Job 10:21; Psalm 143:3; Psalm 115:17). Individuals who go there are literally 'shadows of their former selves'. There are however some ominous references to *Sheol* (Job 21:13; 24:19; Psalm 9:17; Proverbs 5:5). There are also references to God's deliverance from this 'shadowy' place (Psalm 49:15; Psalm 73:24). He was able to make his presence felt even in that dark place (Psalm 139:8).

In the New Testament the Greek word used to translate the Hebrew *Sheol* is *ades* (Hades), meaning 'hidden or unseen'. It may be connected to *aines* (gloomy or gruesome) or *hado* (all receiving). The Greek version of the Old Testament translates *Sheol* into *Hades* sixty-one times out of sixty-five.

In the 400 years between completing the Old Testament writings and the start of the New Testament period the Jews came to believe that *Sheol/Hades* was divided into two parts: one for the wicked and one for the righteous (Luke 16:23–31).

A second word used to translate Sheol is *gehenna* which Jesus used to describe the terrible future prospects of those who die without faith in him (Matthew 5:29; Mark 9:43, 47). John Blanchard writes, '. . . Gehenna, with all its imagery of shame, disgrace, sin and guilt, judgment and punishment is "hell".' (*Whatever happened to Hell?*)

Heaven

Heaven can be translated 'air' or 'sky' (Matthew 6:26; 24:29, 35; Hebrews 11:12). It was created co-operatively by God the Father and God the Son (Revelation 3:14; 10:6) and is the place where God resides (Matthew 5:16; Revelation 3:12). Heaven is the place where the Lord Jesus came from to undertake his ministry on earth (John 3:13, 31). After the resurrection he returned to Heaven, ascending to the highest point (Ephesians 4:10) and sitting down at the right hand side of God the father, the place of power, authority and status (Hebrews 1:8; 1 Peter 3:22). Heaven is also the residence of the angels (Matthew 18:10; 22:30) and is the eternal home of those who place their faith in Christ (2 Corinthians 5:1).

Psalm 7

I have placed my trust in you Lord

Sometimes we feel that we have nowhere to turn except to the Lord. Only in him will we find true security.

We are not sure of the exact background to this psalm, but whatever the circumstances, David feels that he is in real danger (verses 1–2). Perhaps he has been accused of betraying a friend or an ally (verse 4). He vehemently denies this charge and invites punishment from God upon himself if there is the slightest doubt as to his integrity (verses 3–5).

The psalmist then moves from his personal circumstances to issues that affect society at large (verses 6–9). He calls on God to judge the nations (verse 8). He knows that the Lord will make the right decisions concerning each individual because he knows the inner intentions of everyone's heart (verse 9). Doing what is right involves punishing that which is wrong (verse 11). David recognizes that he is dealing with a God who is not to be taken lightly.

The Lord is pictured as a 'mighty warrior' who has the appropriate weapons to deal a death blow to his enemies (verses 12–13). The irony is that it often does not have to come to a show of arms. Those who set traps for others regularly become victims of their own devices (verses 14–16).

The psalm ends with praise to the God who can be relied upon always to do what is best. He has not only the desire to do what is right but also the power to do what is right, for he is far above anyone else (verse 17).

Questions

1. Why do we react so badly when we are falsely accused?
2. Are we as confident as David that God can always be trusted to do what is right? If not why is this?
3. Trace the ways in which sin grows, as described in verses 12–16. Why must we deal with sin before it gets a hold on us? How can we do so?
4. Are we becoming more racist or less as a society? Where does the church stand on 'racial' issues? (See *A black Benjamite*).

A black Benjamite?

We know very little about 'Cush, a Benjamite'. We do know that the tribe of Benjamin (King Saul's tribe) contained some of those who were most opposed to David (see 2 Samuel 16:5ff; 20:1ff). Some have suggested that 'Cush' may refer to someone from the Sudan, and so perhaps a black man. If this is the case it shows that the Hebrews held no colour bar to membership of their tribes. This argument is interesting, though impossible to substantiate.

Psalm 8

How great is our God

Creation is God's gift to us. We need to enjoy it and take care of it.

This psalm seems to generate great enthusiasm among Christians of every generation. C. S. Lewis referred to it as 'this short exquisite lyric'. Derek Kidner is in verbal overdrive when he says 'this psalm is an unsurpassed example of what a hymn should be, celebrating as it does the glory and grace of God'. The reason for these glowing endorsements is the marvellous picture language used by the psalmist to describe both the greatness of God and the grandeur of his creation.

It begins by declaring the greatness of God. His glory is so much more expansive than we could ever imagine. This is so obvious to those who look with childlike wonder, but can be totally missed by individuals who consider themselves too sophisticated to need God (verses 1–2; see also 1 Kings 8:27).

Perhaps David is reflecting on his days as a shepherd. He

51

might have been recalling a time when he laid on his back on a Judaean hillside looking up at the night sky (verses 3–4). He must have been struck by the enormity of space and how tiny he felt in comparison. Set against the vastness of the universe, we live on a planet that is no more than a speck of dust. As Earth's inhabitants we are little more than tiny microbes. With this in mind David was overwhelmed by the thought that God could be interested in, let alone care for, humankind (verses 3–4).

He now makes an incredible statement. In comparison to the enormity of creation, man may be tiny but he is not insignificant. God has given him an elevated position in the created order of things. He has been given both the privilege and the responsibility, under God, to rule on earth. All the animal kingdom is available for him to benefit from and enjoy. This is a sacred trust that should not be abused. Sadly humankind's record of being earth's 'care-takers' has not always been a good one (verses 5–8).

The psalm ends with a restatement of the sentiments of the first line (verse 9). The Great Creator is our loving Lord. His kindly character 'over flows the Heavens and fills the earth' (The Living Bible).

Questions

1. In what ways does modern life stop us simply enjoying God's creation (see Mark 10:13–16)? How can we counteract this?
2. Dr Bruce Waltke calls Psalm 8 'creation set to music'. How much of our church music celebrates God's creation? What more can be done to demonstrate how majestic God is in our worship?
3. Read verses 6–8. How can we apply their teaching to current issues of animal rights and animal welfare?

The Ark

The 'Ark of the Covenant' was also called the 'Ark of the Lord' (Deuteronomy 10:8) and the 'Ark of the Testimony'. It was made to the pattern given to Moses by God. It was a rectangular box that measured 1220 x 760 x 760mm and was covered in gold. It could be carried on four poles inserted through rings at the four corners. The gold-plated lid or 'mercy seat' had two angelic figures (cherubim) on top, with their wings overshadowing the lid. The Ark contained the two tablets of stone with the Law engraved on them, the Testimony (Exodus 25:16, 21; 40:20; Deuteronomy 10:1–5), a pot filled with manna and Aaron's rod (Hebrews 9:4–5).

The 'Ark' was placed inside the tabernacle (originally a movable tent where God met with Moses). There God would live among his people. The 'mercy seat' was the particular place where the Lord chose to appear to Moses and to speak with him (Exodus 25:1–22).

It has been suggested that David wrote this psalm to commemorate the return of the Ark to Jerusalem (see 2 Samuel 6:1–19). The irony is that in doing so he may have taken a Philistine tune and set his own words to it. Years later the founder of the Salvation Army, William Booth, said 'Why should the devil have all the good music?' It could be that we have in the tune for this psalm a very early example of such an approach.

Psalms 9 and 10

In God's academy

Some lessons in life take a long time to learn.

We are going to deal with Psalms 9 and 10 together because they appear to be not two songs but one. There are twenty-two letters in the Hebrew alphabet and in this poem  each new sentence starts with the next letter in sequence – an acrostic. So verse 1 of Psalm 9 begins with the Hebrew equivalent of the letter 'A', verse 2 begins with the Hebrew equivalent to 'B', and so on. This would help people to remember it easily. Psalm 9 has the first half of the Hebrew alphabet and Psalm 10 the second half. The ancient Greek version of the Old Testament, the Septuagint, certainly treats them as if they belong together.

Tragedy

It is evident from the information given in the title that this song was written at a time of personal tragedy. We are not sure whose son had died. It may well have been David's son, Absalom (see 2 Samuel 18). If this was the case it makes the psalm even more poignant. For David had learnt many painful parental lessons because of this son of his. Absalom was what Thackray Eddy called 'a dangerous rascal. He was that most dangerous of rascals, a charming one.' He knew how to use flattery to get his own way. He had even tried to charm the people into turning against his father and giving the kingdom to him (2 Samuel 15:1–37).

In the end, despite his personal charisma, Absalom came to a 'sticky end'. In his haste to escape he became entangled by his long hair on a tree, was captured and subsequently killed (2 Samuel 18:1–15). When David was informed he was completely devastated (2 Samuel 18:33). Absalom may have caused his father much grief with his antics while he was alive but this was nothing to compare with the anguish brought about by his untimely death.

Some scholars suggest that the death referred to in the title was not Absalom but a son of King David's friend. Whatever the case, the death of a child is a bitter experience and a hard one to come to terms with.

Praise in times of pain

Incredibly in his time of pain David is able to praise God (verses 1–2). His focus is not on the awful events but on God, the One who is able to perform 'wonders'. Like Job he has learnt how to praise the Lord even in the face of death (Job 13:15). David recognizes that God is above everything, he is the 'Most High' (verse 2). Even death itself is nothing in comparison with his power (1 Corinthians 15:54–57).

If death is not to be feared then neither are David's enemies (verses 3–6). It is not death or enemies that control events but the Lord who is in charge. This is the God who can be trusted always to make the right decisions and to look after the weak and the oppressed (verses 7–10).

This leads David to begin a song of praise (verse 11), for he knows that God will always have a listening ear for those who are in trouble (verse 12). Here he is continuing to learn the lesson that praise and prayer must be constant companions. The enemies, though not as powerful as God, are still a real problem for him (verse 13). He asks God to rescue him so that he may continue to praise him (verse 14). The psalmist's prayer could be seen to be answered in that the nations that set traps for him often find themselves victims of their own treachery. This awesome outworking of the righteous judgments of God causes David to tell his readers to stop and think about the implications of this for a moment (verses 15–16). The word *Higgaion* may be an instruction for the musicians to play quietly here. The word *Selah* may have been added to encourage quiet meditation on what has been said (see comments on Psalm 3).

One step forward, two steps back

The psalmist returns to the sad subject of those nations which choose to conduct their affairs without reference to God. This can only result in tragedy. For while God will always help those who turn to him in time of need (verse 18), he will prove that in the final analysis he is the One who will win. Indeed David prays for this to happen in order that it might shake the unbelieving nations to the core (verses 19–20).

The Psalms reflect accurately that God's people often take one step forward and two steps back. As Psalm 10 begins, David again expresses his frustration at the apparent inactivity of God (verse 1). Believing that God is involved in the events of the world when all the evidence seems to deny this is a hard lesson to learn.

He is having a particular problem with the fact that those who live without reference to God seem to be doing so well. These arrogant people appear to go out of their way to hurt others. Ronald Allen describes them as those who 'strut their stuff with a haughtiness that seems as limitless as their own evil horizons'. They are generally obnoxious, boasting about their achievements and outrageously thumbing their noses at God. Yet he appears not to mind, for he seems to ignore it (verses 2–11).

David calls on God to show his hand (verse 12). He asks him to intervene and help those who cannot help themselves. The psalmist believes that the boasts of the arrogant unbelievers will ultimately prove false, for in the end their power base will be broken (verse 15). For David has learned from personal experience that God does care for his extended family despite the outward circumstances that seem to speak to the contrary (verse 14).

The psalm concludes with a declaration that in God we have a King who really cares for his subjects (verses 16–18). David has learned some important lessons in God's academy of life.

Questions

1. Why is it appropriate to praise God in the middle of painful experiences (see Acts 16:22–34 and 1 Thessalonians 5:16–17)?
2. How do we deal with periods in our church's life when God 'appears' to be inactive?
3. How should Christians react to 'arrogant atheism' (see Psalm 10:4)?

Psalm 11

Dealing with discouragement

'Running away' is not the way to deal with discouragement.

A car bumper sticker read 'Since I've given up hope I feel much better!' These sentiments would fit well the mood we find David in at the beginning of this psalm. For it seems that he has been going through a difficult and discouraging time.

Added to this was the depressing advice he was receiving from some of his so-called friends that the only way to deal with his difficulties was to run away. These advisers were really painting a gloomy picture. They were telling him to run for it, but he would probably still get shot down anyway! These 'gloom mongers' continued with their litany of woe by saying that the situation was totally hopeless and nothing could be done about it.

David recognizes that no-one can run away from their problems. For, like our shadows on a sunny day, problems tend to follow us wherever we go. So he speaks to his faint-hearted friends and tells them that in times of trouble the best thing to do is to take refuge in God, and not to run away (verses 1–3).

Refuge in God

David is able to find protection in God because the Lord is in control of the universe and in touch with human affairs. He knows in fine detail all that is happening here on earth (verse 4). He not only keeps a close eye on those who do the right thing, he also closely scrutinizes those who choose to do the wrong thing. These people will not escape his judgment (verses 5–6).

The psalm ends with some encouraging words. David is lifted by the thought that God can be trusted always to do what is just and fair. He also expresses his confidence that those who live lives of integrity will meet with God face to face (verse 7).

Questions

1. What kinds of people tend to discourage you? How can we counteract discouragement?
2. What kinds of issues tend to discourage local churches? Again, how can we counteract this together?
3. Well-meaning friends can often give us the wrong advice (see Matthew 16:22). How are we to test advice to see if it is really the right thing to do?

4. How can we know that the situation in the world is never totally hopeless? How can we share the hope that we have with those who need it most?

Psalm 12

Words can never hurt me?

Our words can be used to hurt or heal.

We have all heard the children's taunt 'sticks and stones may break my bones but words can never hurt me'. Most of us have proved it to be patently untrue. Words can hurt, in fact words can be used as tools of destruction. The tongue can be a lethal weapon (see James 3:1–11).

This psalm is all about the use and abuse of words. David makes a desperate plea to God for help because it appears that all signs of godly living have vanished from society (verse 1). Everybody's words seem 'hollow', there is no ring of truth about anything that is being said (verse 2; the word 'lies' translates the Hebrew word for 'hollowness'). There is a lot of 'flattery', people are using words to get what they want out of each other.

David recognizes that God is not impressed with people who try to manipulate others with 'smooth' speech. He asks the Lord to 'shut the mouths' (literally 'cut off the lips') of those who seek to use flattery in order to advance themselves. These are over-confident people who depend on their 'gift of the gab' to get them through life. They need to be stopped and David prays that this may happen (verses 3–4).

His prayer evokes a response from heaven. God agrees to

intervene on behalf of the needy. He promises to protect the weak from those who attempt to overpower them with words. In contrast to those who use words to try to gain an advantage over others, God's words are trustworthy and pure (verses 5–6).

The psalm concludes with a prayer for protection. God's help is always needed when society is sick. The way words are used is always evidence of the true health of a civilization (verse 8).

Questions

1. How can we guard against using our words to hurt, and remind ourselves to use them to heal?
2. Read what James says about the tongue in James 3:1–12. What does our use of the tongue say about the kind of people we are?
3. Why do we tend to use words as weapons during conflicts in the local church?
4. Who should we trust to speak the 'truth' in our society?

Psalm 13

O Lord where are you?

When there seems no end to our problems we can feel forgotten by God.

The title of the psalm tells us who wrote it, but we cannot be quite so certain about when it was written. It may have been penned against the backdrop of David's life on the

run from King Saul (see 1 Samuel 18ff). This campaign was a war of nerves and could have continued for months, if not years. Whatever the trouble was that caused him to write such a heart-wrenching psalm, it was the ongoing nature of the problem which caused him so much pain.

Singing the blues

The Psalms contain all the music of the human heart. Here David begins by singing the blues. The reason for this is that he feels that God has forgotten him (verses 1–2). This is the experience of a believer and it demonstrates that there is no immunity from the icy fingers of doubt even for the people of God.

We know that the Bible teaches us that God is able to forget sin which has been confessed and repented of (Jeremiah 31:34). But does God ever forget about his saints? Can he be 'absent minded' where his people are concerned? David certainly seems to be suggesting just that!

How did the psalmist reach this conclusion? He feels forgotten because of the duration of his problem. This point is brought home to us by the repeated use of the phrase 'How long' (literally 'until when'), which occurs four times in this short psalm (verses 1–2). He also feels forgotten by God because he no longer senses his presence. God seems to be hiding from him (verse 1). This sense of God's distance from him stirs up some deep emotions in his soul. He is in mental turmoil, wrestling with his thoughts. Dark thoughts and depressing moods seem to have been his constant companions (verse 2). Added to this mental trauma is the fact that he is also in turmoil physically (verse 4). His enemies are moving in for the kill. They are boasting about their victory over him. Mentally, spiritually, emotionally and physically David has his back against the wall. What can he do in such a situation? He prays!

A cry for help

There are two parts to his prayer (verses 3–4). Firstly David asks God simply to take notice of him and answer his request (verse 3). He uses the word 'LORD' to remind himself that he is praying to a God who always keeps his promises. The term 'LORD' translates the Hebrew word *Yahweh* which speaks of God's covenant-keeping character.

The second part of the prayer is a desperate cry for help. The phrase 'Give light to my eyes, or I will sleep in death' (verse 3) comes straight from the battlefield. It was the cry of a dying soldier calling out for someone to come to his aid. Like a dying man David calls out to God to help him.

We do not know whether God changed David's circumstances or whether he gave him extra strength to cope. Charles Swindoll is convinced that it was David who underwent change and not his circumstances. He writes,

> David often begins his psalms at the bottom of the valley and by the time the song is over he is at the top of the mountain. The amazing thing is that it only took him maybe a day or two to write the psalm. What changed? David changed. His circumstances didn't. And he's singing the hymn at the end of the psalm even though his circumstances are unchanged. (Charles Swindoll, *Stress fractures. Coping with today's pressures* (Scripture Press, 1990) pp. 46–7)

What is abundantly clear from the psalm is that David has moved from trauma to trust and that this has been brought about by prayer.

Now the atmosphere changes from despair to delight (verses 5–6). David has gone through desolation (verses 1–4) to supplication and prayer (verse 3) and on to adoration (verses 5–6).

He ends the song with worship which springs out of his trust in God's constant love. His joy is established upon the certainty of God's salvation. All this leads David to burst into song which has as its theme the goodness of God (verse 6).

Questions

1. What kinds of circumstances tend to make us feel that we have been forgotten by God? How have you come through these times in the past?
2. As a Christian community, how can we help those in our local church who feel that God has abandoned them? How can we ensure that they have opportunities to say how they feel, without fear of condemnation?
3. How would you reply to someone who said, 'If there is a God he isn't concerned about this world. He doesn't do anything to stop disasters'?

God's forgetfulness

Does God ever forget us? Read Isaiah 49:14–16. Here God reminds his people that he will not forget them. His hands are marked as a reminder!

In the New Testament Jesus' disciples thought that once he had gone back to heaven he would forget about them. But Jesus promised that he would not only remember them but that he would return for them (see John 14:1–3). Like his Father, Jesus also has marked hands to remind him of his people!

David discovered that he could praise God in every situation. This is a lesson all believers have to learn sooner or later (see Daniel 3:16; Isaiah 43:1–3; Acts 16:25; Philippians 4:4–6; 1 Thessalonians 5:16–17).

Psalm 14

Wisdom, from Heaven's perspective

'Foolishness' is living as if God does not exist.

It is striking that in our culture people are often thought to be wise, not on the basis of what they affirm, but on the basis of what they deny. For example, it may be considered  the correct intellectual approach to deny the existence of God. Many people were doing so in David's day and many continue to do so today (verse 1).

A fool by name and nature

The psalmist responds to such thinking. He considers it utterly foolish (verse 1). The Hebrew word translated 'fool' is *nabal*. This describes a person who is not simply misguided but determined to pursue the wrong course of action (see 1 Samuel 25:25, where Nabal was seen to be a fool by name and by nature). Dr Garry Inrig describes the 'fool' as 'an individual who makes choices as if God does not exist and who lives as if God has not spoken' (Luke 12:13–21). To be a 'fool' in God's perspective is to have missed the very point of life. The person who acts this way is not reaching the heights of wisdom but plumbing the depths of folly (Romans 1:22).

There is so much around us that points to the existence of God (see Psalm 19) that to ignore all the evidence is not an error of judgment but a matter of choice (see Romans 1:18–32). Derek Kidner calls this resistance to belief in God an 'irresponsible gesture of defiance'.

God's assessment of those who deliberately choose not to believe in him is blunt and to the point. They are rotten to the core (verse 1). The word translated 'corrupt' (verses 2 and 3) could equally be rendered 'gone putrid'.

In words of great sadness on God's part, verse 2 describes his futile surveillance of the earth to discover whether there are any hearts turned toward heaven (that is, people seeking after God). His sad conclusion is that there appears to be little interest on earth concerning spiritual things. There seems to be a spiritual principle here. History shows that individuals and societies that choose to turn their backs on God soon begin to turn their backs on goodness (verse 3, see also Romans 1:18 – 2:4; 3:10–12).

When will they ever learn?

David now asks a question that could well be asked by any exasperated parent of delinquent children, 'when will they ever learn?' (verse 4). In the end these individuals' actions will lead them into a cul-de-sac of 'fear' (literally 'terror', see Psalm 53:5; Isaiah 2:19ff; Revelation 6:15) and ultimately God's judgment (verse 5). C. S. Lewis speaks of an appointment with God that no-one, even those who claim not to believe in God, can avoid. He writes, 'In the end that face which is the delight or the terror of the universe must be turned upon each of us'.

Those who hate God and his people will not win out in the final analysis. Those who place their faith in him can count on both his presence and his protection (verses 5–6).

The psalmist ends this song with a prayer that God would mount a rescue plan for his people (verse 7). These words were a heart cry from God's people in David's day and they are still on the lips of believers today. As Christians we look forward with anticipation to the return of Jesus (1 Corinthians 16:22).

Questions

---

1. Do you agree that those of us who call ourselves Christians sometimes live as if God does not exist? How does this manifest itself?
2. If believing in God is more a matter of choice than an intellectual debate, how should this affect our approach to evangelism?
3. Read Romans 1:18–32 and 3:10–12. What happens when God gives people over to their folly? What evidence of this can you see in our own society?

Psalm 15

Who can live close to you Lord?

Belief and behaviour must go together.

What we believe must make an impact on how we behave. This is how we must live if we are not to have the charge of being hypocritical levelled against us. As God's people we are called to live lives of integrity. It really does matter what we are like when no-one is looking! This psalm brings together belief and behaviour in an unbreakable partnership.

Danger: holy object!

It could be that David has been meditating on the events depicted in 2 Samuel 6:12–19 and 1 Chronicles 13:1–13. That was the occasion when David brought the Ark of the Covenant from the house of Obed-Edom to the 'City of David' and placed it in a tent specially built to contain it. Unfortunately during the journey the oxen which were pulling the cart on which the Ark was being transported stumbled. In an effort to save it from falling to the ground, Uzzah reached out to steady the Ark with his hands. He was immediately struck down dead! The narrative explains why this took place. It was 'because of his irreverent act' (2 Samuel 6:7). This incident made a lasting impression on David. He must have felt partially to blame for Uzzah's death. He knew that the Ark was to be carried by priests and Levites and should not have been on the back of a cart. To some extent his negligence had brought about this tragedy (Exodus 25:12–15; Numbers 4:15; Joshua 3:14). It was a lesson he would not quickly forget (1 Chronicles 15:2). This experience may well be the background to the writing of Psalms 15 and 24.

In the light of the awesome holiness of God, who can approach him, let alone live close to him? David seeks to answer this question which he poses at the beginning of the psalm (verse 1).

Holy life

In verses 2–5 he describes the qualities required of people wishing to live close to God. As soon as these are laid out it is immediately obvious that only the Lord Jesus was able to live such a life. The next logical conclusion is that only a person who is 'in-Christ' (2 Corinthians 5:17) could possibly ever begin to live like this!

These people are going to live a 'blameless' life (verse 2). This does not mean an absolutely perfect life. The Lord Jesus is the only human to have walked through the pages of human history without ever sinning (Hebrews 4:15). What it does seem to mean is that these people give themselves wholeheartedly and without mixed motives to the service of God and others.

To live a life that is pleasing to God we have not only to know what is right but also do what is right (verse 2). What is

67

required here is not only to do the right thing but also to do it in the right way.

It is important that godly people can be trusted always to say what they mean and mean what they say; in other words to speak the truth, the whole truth and nothing but the truth (verse 2, see also Matthew 5:33–37).

There are always positives and negatives about living a godly life. There are things that we must do (verse 2) and things that we must not do (verses 3–5). According to both David and Paul there must not be a hint of malicious talk in the lives of believers (verse 3, see also Ephesians 5:4). They will not want to engage in spreading rumours or in using words deliberately to damage another's reputation. Rather, like Jesus, they will want to speak the truth graciously and in love (John 1:17; Ephesians 4:17–32).

We may be called to live gentle lives but we are not expected to be gullible. Godly people have to make right assessments about those who are living in accordance with God's Laws and those who are not (verse 4).

It won't be easy to live this way. There will be no soft options as far as honouring commitments is concerned (verse 4). The individual who wants to stay close to God must not be anxious to get rich at any cost. Becoming a 'loan-shark' or a 'bribe taker' is not a valid career move for believers (verse 5).

This kind of life not only will please God and lead to closeness to God, but will also result in a stable personality (verse 5).

Questions

1. How do we live when we are not among Christian friends? Why is it important that Christians live lives of integrity?
2. How can we support each other in our church as we endeavour to live holy lives in our society?
3. Should we object to 'bad language' wherever it is found? How can we object in a way that will lead to witness rather than arguments?

Psalm 16

Protect me Lord!

The only good thing about our lives is what the Lord has done.

 Woody Allen said, 'The future is not what it used to be.' This psalm is concerned with what lies ahead (verses 9–11). Those who live without reference to God have every reason to worry about the future. David, however, is fully persuaded that the God who has kept him safe in the past, will keep him safe in the future (see 2 Timothy 1:12).

He is able to pray with confidence about his security because he had personally proved God's protection in the past (verse 1). His faith is not at a distance, it is up close and personal ('You are *my* God', verse 2). He trusts God because he knows God.

God helps those who can't help themselves

This faith of David's is not the kind that has for its motto 'the Lord helps those who help themselves'. He recognizes that he is totally dependent on God and that apart from the Lord there is nothing good about his life (verse 2, see also John 15:5).

He is not exclusive about his faith. He knows that God has a special place in his heart for all his people ('saints', verse 3).

While he considers the pleasure that God's people bring to their Lord, David notes the pain that waits for those who turn their backs on God (verse 4). Even to mention these sad people is difficult (verse 4). He certainly has no intention of joining them in their folly (verse 4).

Count your blessings

The psalmist now begins to count his blessings (verses 5–6). God has met all his physical needs for food, drink and housing (verse 5). More than this, he has provided many delightful bonuses as well (verse 6).

God has also taken care of him spiritually. He has given David much-needed counsel and helped him to make the right decisions (verse 7). As he looks back David concludes that his past policy of always seeking first God's kingdom ('I have set the LORD always before me'; verse 8, see also Matthew 6:33), will serve him well in the future. In this way he will stand secure ('I will not be shaken', verse 8).

Not only are his past and present taken care of but his future is secure as well (verses 9–11). Even in death he can rest assured that God will be there for him (verse 10). To be in the presence of the God you love is the source of real joy, whether it be in this life or the life to come (verse 11).

Questions

---

1. Why do we worry about the future? Why do we find it difficult to trust God about it?
2. What grounds do Christians have to enjoy life? What stops us doing so?
3. What does society understand by the word 'joy'? How can we point to true joy without giving the impression that the Christian life is a bed of roses?

Future hope

In regard to verses 10–11 John Stott has suggested there are three levels of interpretation open to us, all of which are true.

1. Literally these verses express David's confidence that he will not die; his soul will not be delivered 'into the power of death'. We do not know the exact historical background to this psalm, but it could be referring to those months 'on the run' from Saul when David was in daily danger of death. In this psalm, then, David was expressing his unshakeable confidence in God's ability to keep him alive.

2. These verses could refer to enjoying 'eternal life'. For the believer eternal life begins, not when we die, but when we become Christians. In these verses we have a picture of the pleasure we can experience living in the presence of God. This is a pleasure that not even death can interrupt. Of course David had only a part of the full picture. The fuller understanding of 'eternal life' had to wait for the coming of Christ (see 2 Timothy 1:10). Because of Christ's victory over death (1 Corinthians 15:57) the believer not only enjoys the Lord's presence in this life but in the life to come (John 14:1–3; Philippians 1:21–23).

3. When the writers of the New Testament read these verses they were not slow in applying them to the resurrection of the Lord Jesus Christ (Acts 2:30, 31; 1 Peter 1:10–12).

Psalm 17

Demonstrate your great love O Lord

Some parts of life are private.

Our faith in God does have some elements which are very private. Prayer is one area which certainly does have a personal and private side to it (Matthew 6:5–6).

In this regard we need to approach this particular psalm with sensitivity. Here we are observing a godly person engaged in a period of personal prayer.

Pray in line with the will of God

David begins his prayer time by asking God to pay attention to him (verse 1). At first he appears to be approaching God on the basis of his own righteousness (verse 1, 'Hear, O LORD my *righteous* plea'). If we look a little closer, however, we can see that it is the 'rightness' of his request that is the thrust of his words. He is coming before God to ask for action over an issue which he believes to be in line with the will of God (see Romans 8:26–27). He is not trying to deceive God, his prayer 'does not rise from deceitful lips' (verse 1). That would be impossible and therefore a waste of energy. He is simply convinced that God can be trusted to do the right thing and so prove that David is a man of integrity (verse 2).

Examine your inner motives

David has the utmost confidence that even if God made a detailed examination of his inner motives, nothing devious would be found. He has resolved to have nothing whatsoever to do with dishonest speech (verse 3). There is nothing underhand about David's intentions and there is nothing dangerous about his actions (verse 4). He has resolutely stuck to God's path even when the temptation came to take a short cut (verse 5).

Pray with confidence

We now get to the heart of David's prayer (verses 6–15). He approaches God with confidence that he will be heard in heaven (verse 6, see also Hebrews 4:16). He asks God to demonstrate the awesome power of his great love and to display his saving intervention in human history (verse 7).

This psalm shows us a man who is in a close relationship with God and wants this to continue. He wants to know God personally and to know his protection (verses 8–9). To be protected by God does not mean that we will avoid all troubles in life. It does mean that we can be assured of God's presence in times of trouble (Isaiah 43:1–3).

David knew that there were those who were literally 'out to get' him, whether with their words or their violent actions (verses 10–11). These people were always looking for an opportunity to pounce on an unsuspecting victim (verse 12).

David boldly asks God to deal with his enemies. He pictures the Lord as a mighty warrior wielding a sword of destruction (verse 13). Almost as an aside he notes that his enemies have a shortsighted view of life. They focus only on this world and not on the rewards offered by the next (verse 14).

To finish his prayer and the psalm David ends with praising God for his provision. He has met all his practical needs. One day God will satisfy his deepest desire, that of meeting with him face to face (verse 15, see also 1 Corinthians 13:12).

Questions

1. Why is it important to spend time in 'private prayer'? How can we make it a priority in our own routines?
2. How can we encourage one another, in our churches, to stay close to God? What most helps you to do so?
3. Where does the world look for security? What makes these places inadequate?
4. In this psalm, David shows his confidence in God's character and promises. How should our lives show this confidence?

Psalm 18

Passion and power!

God loves us enough to protect us. He is powerful enough to guarantee our ultimate safety.

This psalm's title indicates that it was written by David when he found time to rest after defeating his enemies. While reflecting on past victories, David's mind turns toward God and his faithfulness.  Before long his heart is taken up with all that the Lord means to him. A song of praise was sure to follow. Psalm 18 was the result of David's reflection and rejoicing.

The psalm itself is very similar to the song of praise we find in 2 Samuel 22. It is also introduced by a similar historical reference. This substantial song keeps up its pace and vibrancy right the way through.

God our protector

It begins with words that communicate both passion and power. David obviously loves God with all his heart and with all his might. The reason for such strength of feeling on his part was that God had proved to be such a strong protector. The metaphors he uses, such as, 'rock', 'fortress', 'refuge' and 'shield' underline this. God not only protects and liberates, he also empowers ('horn' is used here as a symbol of strength (verses 1–2).

He is worthy of extravagant praise because of the great care he has shown to David (verse 3).

God in a crisis

David continues to reflect upon all that God has done for him. He remembers a time of terrible testing he had to pass through when he felt his circumstances had him in what amounted to 'a death-grip' (verse 4). He felt overwhelmed by what was going on. Like a drowning man he was struggling to stay afloat (verses 4–5).

In this time of crisis he turned to the Lord in prayer. God responded to his desperate cry for help in a most dramatic way (verse 6)! It seems that David has proved the truth of the saying that 'our extremities are often God's opportunities'. For when he felt that he was powerless to do anything, God demonstrated that he was powerful enough to do anything.

The psalmist struggles here to find words to do justice to his experience. The phrases are carefully chosen to describe this 'close encounter of a divine kind'. He employs picture words to convey God's power (verse 7), God's purity (verse 8), swiftness to intervene (verses 9–10), and awe-inspiring nature (verses 11–15).

God's power to save

This show of great power is not an end in itself. The intention was to rescue the struggling psalmist. All God's resources were brought to bear on this one important operation (verse 16). The

Lord's strength contrasted with David's weakness. He could not save himself, only God could rescue him, only God could keep him safe (verses 17–18). There is an added bonus here. Not only had the Lord saved him from a terrible fate but he generously situated him in a delightful setting (verse 19). All this was a testimony to God's delight in his servant.

In the next verses David does appear to be depending on his own self-effort to make himself right with God (verses 20–24). Perhaps we can best understand this by recognizing that this is more a matter of intent, rather than a constant reality. We know that he did not always keep God's laws (see 2 Samuel 11–12). He did commit sins and he knew it (see Psalm 32 and Psalm 51). What we have here is the psalmist declaring that he is attempting always to do God's will. He is appealing to God to honour this intent. John Calvin believed that these verses spoke more about the Lord Jesus than they did of David. In the final analysis only he could keep all God's laws perfectly.

God is faithful

David now moves on to the subject of 'great truths about God' (verses 25–27). God is always faithful to those who are faithful to him. He always shows his absolute purity to those who live pure lives. He is always ready to help those who admit that they cannot help themselves. But he also knows when someone is crooked and proud of it, and he will ensure that such a person is punished for it.

In times of darkness David had proved that the Lord was his searchlight, showing him the way (verse 28). In times of weakness he had proved that the Lord was his supply of strength which enabled him to do extraordinary feats (verse 29).

This was the kind of God David believed in, this was the Lord he worshipped. His deeds are always perfect; his words are always faultless; his protection is beyond comparison (verses 30–31). Encouraged by these thrilling aspects of God's character, he returns to reflecting on God's protective care of him (verses 32–45).

The psalm ends with another surge of praise to God for all that he is and all that he has done. David has proved that the Lord is 'rock solid'. He not only saves, but keeps (verses 46–50).

Questions

1. How often do you reflect on all that God has done in your life? What benefits are there in doing so?
2. In our churches how can we encourage one another to depend on the Lord to show us what step to take next?
3. Society often seems to be floundering in 'deep waters' (verse 16). Why does it stay floundering? What is the way out?

Psalm 19

God's glory revealed

Creation shouts out loud. There is a God!

This poem is considered by many to be among the finest in the entire collection. C. S. Lewis once wrote: 'This is the greatest poem in the Psalter (the book of Psalms) and one of the greatest lyrics in the world'.

God's majesty

It has a certain dignity and splendour about it. The song begins with a magnificent panorama of the night sky. As David reflects upon the vastness of the star-filled heavens, his thoughts cannot help but turn to the majesty of God (see Psalm 8).

Not only is he taken up with the sights of the starry sky, but also with the sounds issuing from space. It seems that he does not believe that space is silent. Indeed it is quite the reverse, it is shouting out a message! The glorious nature of the heavens speaks of the greater glory of the One who had created them (verse 1).

The heavens testify to God's existence and greatness. For David this is too obvious to be ignored. God's creation speaks regularly to those who listen and his message can be received anywhere on the planet (verses 2–4). There is, therefore, no excuse for a person who claims not to believe in God. His creation acts like a megaphone announcing a clear message that God is there. It's not that people can't hear, but that they choose not to accept the evidence that creation offers. To ignore the facts is a foolish and fatal misjudgment (see Psalm 14 and Romans 1:20).

David turns from the sky at night to the full blaze of the sun-filled day (verses 5–6). Again he is staggered by the greatness of God. He recognizes that the earth depends on the awesome power of the sun. The sun, however, is no more than a tool in the hand of God. As G. K. Chesterton put it, 'every morning God tells it to get up, and it does'.

God's Word

In the next part of this psalm the writer turns from the idea of God revealing himself through nature, to his revelation through his Word (verses 7–11). He enthuses about the qualities of God's Word, or as it is called here 'God's Law'.

He tells us that God's Word is perfect, complete in every way. He also informs us that if we listen to it our whole being will be refreshed and revived (verse 7). God's Word invigorates those who pay attention to it. It also can be trusted to give wisdom, guidance and joy to those who make it a part of their life. There is no more valuable a commodity than God's Word. It is to be treasured above the most precious metals, and to be sought after like the finest foods (verse 10).

At this point David begins to look closely at himself. He finds that the Word of God reveals that he too is far from perfect (verses 12–13). He begins to pray that those areas of his life that were not in accordance with God's revealed will might be dealt with. He asks God to forgive those sins which were unplanned, not deliberate. But there is a more serious issue at stake here. He also needs God's help if he is to avoid what the Old Testament calls 'sin with a high hand' (see Numbers 15:30; Deuteronomy 1:43; 17:12, 13). These are the sins we commit deliberately. We know what is the right thing to do and still we perversely choose to do what is wrong. David is confident that with God's strength he can live a life free from blame (verse 13).

The psalm ends with a prayer that preachers have used down the ages. What really counts is that we all handle God's Word in a way that pleases its author (verse 14).

Questions

1. Think of some ways in which creation 'speaks' to you about God? What does it tell you?
2. Think about your church's life and worship. How much emphasis is there on teaching God's Word? How could your church make more opportunities to learn from the Bible together? What place do we give in our churches to teaching God's Word?
3. The world is seldom convinced by creation's testimony. Why do you think this is?

Making wise the simple

Dr Bob Gorden has the following helpful comments to make about the phrase 'making wise the simple' (verse 7). He writes:
For the Psalmist there was no question of the word of God

being a dead thing. It came to him full of power and life; indeed it was the essential reviving influence of his inner being. It came to him as the word of wisdom. Wisdom here is not something esoteric and theoretical. When the Scripture tells us that the statutes of the Lord make wise the simple, it is showing those who understand it something very important. The 'simple' are a very significant class of people in the Old Testament. They are those who are open to anything. They are not closed to God and his ways but they might be just as open to other influences. They are *very impressionable and easily lead*. In this sense they have no wisdom. God's word has the power to change all that. It comes with revealing and directing power. It is no mere word of advice, bland in character and open-ended in nature. It carries within it the power of change and the way of life.

(*Personally Speaking* (Sovereign Word, 1995))

Psalm 20

My prayer for you

We should always pray before any battle!

When it comes to prayer, Dr Alan Redpath had the following advice, 'Let us keep our chins up and our knees down – we're on the victory side!' This positive and prayerful approach is in keeping with the spirit of this psalm.

Here we have a prayer that was designed to be used before going into battle. Psalm 20 can be offered before entering any testing time, while Psalm 21 is a song of praise to be sung after the battle is over.

The psalm begins with a request that those who are about to enter a difficult time might know God's help and support (verse 1). David encourages those who are entering the battle to trust in the Lord who has always protected his people. From the days of their ancestor Jacob, God has never let his people down. He can be trusted to take care of them now (verse 1).

Remember what God has done

David encourages his companions to look back to see what God has done for them in the past and encourages them to expect his help in the present difficulty. 'Sanctuary' and 'Zion' speak of the place where God's special presence can be experienced. To know God is especially with us is essential when times are tough (verse 2). David has encouraged his friends to remember what God has done for them. He now moves on to the hope that God will remember all that his people have done for him (verse 3). A commitment to living sacrificially is never a waste of time as far as God is concerned. The hours of sacrificial prayer do not go unnoticed in heaven.

God loves to give

The psalmist is not one of those people who believe that God's favourite word to us is 'No!' He is convinced that God is a kind Father who delights to give good gifts to his children (see Luke 11:11–13). God wants our plans and strategies to succeed; he wants us to be on the winning side (verse 4). When the victory is won, then the celebrations can begin (verse 5).

The most powerful person in the kingdom in those days was the king. In Israel, however, the kings always had to recognize that they were put in their place of power and privilege by God, not by their own efforts. David recognized his dependence on God for everything. It was not by the weapons of war that he would succeed, but by trusting in a God who answers prayer and has ultimate power (verses 6–8).

The last verse may be the response of those who first heard this prayer of David. They had heard his prayer for them. Now they have responded in a heartfelt prayer for him (verse 9).

Questions

1. What basis do you have, in the Bible and in your own experience, for believing that prayer changes things?
2. When your church is going through a tough time how can you pray more effectively about the situation?
3. How can we help the world to see that God answers prayer?

The name of the LORD

The 'name of the LORD' refers to all that goes to make up his character (verse 1, see Exodus 3:13–14). The New Testament also speaks of 'the name' of the Lord (John 14:13–14; 17:11–12; Acts 3:6; Revelation 3:12). The followers of Jesus were given the name of Christ – Christians (literally meaning 'little Christs': Acts 11:25). Although it was used first as a term of ridicule, it came to mean that they were to be so identified with Jesus that their lifestyle would cause others to recognize that they belonged to him.

Burnt offerings

The Hebrew word translated 'burnt offerings' denotes 'that which ascends, that is, in smoke to God, being wholly reduced to ashes'. It refers to an offering that was totally burnt up. It first appears in Genesis and is the only form of sacrifice mentioned in that book (Genesis 8:20; 15:9; 22:2, 7, 8, 13). Later, the priests made these offerings on behalf of themselves and the people (see Leviticus 1:9; 9:7, 16, 17). They were offered daily, at major festivals and on special occasions (Exodus 29:38–42), and also when a priest was consecrated to God's service (Exodus 29:15). Burnt offerings were made after a significant event had taken place in the history of the people of God: for example, after the Flood (Genesis 8:20), or after a special revelation of God (Genesis 22:13; Judges 13:16). They were also made before taking on a risky enterprise or encountering a particularly dangerous enemy (Judges 6:23–26; 1 Samuel 26:19).

Psalm 21

Rejoice!

When God does something in our lives our attitude should be one of gratitude.

As we have seen Psalm 20 was David's prayer before a great battle. There he prayed that God would protect both his troops and himself (Psalm 20:1). Psalm 21 was written in the aftermath of that battle when victory had been achieved. If Psalm 20 was a song of prayer, then Psalm 21 is a song of praise.

God's generosity

The psalm begins with the recognition that it was through God's power that the battle was won (verse 1). This brought great joy to David because the Lord had granted every request he had made (verse 2).

He continues with this theme of God's generosity. God has been good to him in so many ways. David has been given the privilege of leading the people of God as their earthly king. The mention of the 'crown of pure gold' in verse 3 speaks more about David's estimation of the Giver than about the value of the gift.

There are some things, however, which are more valuable than gold. The psalmist knows that it is only by the grace of God that he has come through the battle unharmed. There is a strong indication here that he is referring to a quality of life and joy that goes beyond the grave (verses 4–6). Again we have to recognize that a more complete understanding of the concept of eternal life was not available until the New Testament period (see comments on Psalm 16).

God's dependability

David is able to declare his absolute trust in God because he has proved in his own life that the Lord can be depended upon. That goes for even the most testing times, when everything around seems to be unstable. He is confident that he will stand secure (verse 7, 'he will not be shaken'). In the final analysis it is the Lord, not David, who will deal with those who threaten the people of God (verses 8–12).

The psalm concludes with David encouraging his listeners to join him in worship and praise. He believes that God's strength and power are worth singing about (verse 13).

Questions

━━

1. Can you think of times when you have taken for granted what God has done for you? If we felt as grateful as we should, how would this affect our lives?

2. How should our gratitude to God be reflected in our worship services? Discuss whether your church strikes the right balance between thanksgiving, asking God for things and teaching.
3. Our society often emphasizes 'me first' rather than generosity. What impact could Christians make if we really followed God's pattern for generosity? Why are we hesitant to be 'too generous'?

Psalm 22

Deserted by God?

——————

Sometimes we feel totally abandoned by God.

Psalm 22 is the first of a group of three psalms which Christians have traditionally understood to speak prophetically about the Lord Jesus Christ (Psalms 22, 23, 24). These songs contain insights into three aspects of the work of Christ. They give details concerning his suffering for his people (Psalm 22), his shepherding of his people (Psalm 23) and his sovereign rule over his people (Psalm 24).

Before we look at these three psalms in detail, we need to remind ourselves that they were written originally to describe the writer's own personal circumstances. It is the wonder of God's inspired Word that these same songs can so accurately be applied to the life of Christ. The New Testament writers had no doubt that these psalms referred to the Lord Jesus.

A song for the lonely heart

The title of this psalm may indicate that it was to be accompanied by music which fitted the theme of extreme loneliness. Some scholars have suggested that 'The Doe of the Morning' was a melody about a deer that had become separated from the rest of the herd. If this is the case then the tune would be most appropriate for the words which are to follow.

It goes without saying that David had a firm belief in the existence of God. He knew that it was utter foolishness to deny his existence (Psalm 14:1). What he is saying is that he knows God is real, but he feels that he is standing at a distance. He appears to be experiencing what some have called 'God-forsakenness'. Even his prayers do not seem to be getting through to God. Believers of every generation have told of times when they feel as if the heavens were made of impenetrable brass. They speak of times when their prayers seem to hit the ceiling and go no further.

C. S. Lewis tells of such a time in his life. When his wife was dying of cancer he records that he often tried to pray but heaven seemed to be 'bolted shut against him'. Here David felt abandoned, left alone to cope with terrible circumstances and events (verses 1–2). Centuries later a young man dying on a cross was to utter the same words (Matthew 27:46; Mark 15:34).

In the middle of his suffering David suddenly begins to reflect back on the history of God's people. They had proved that God was faithful. The generations of individuals who had placed their lives in his hands had never been disappointed (verse 4).

He hardly has time to steady himself emotionally before the next wave of depressive thoughts begins to sweep over him. He feels that his life really counts for nothing. He appears to have been suffering from an extreme bout of 'self devaluation' (verse 6). The situation is aggravated by the unkind words and actions of some of those around him. These people tease him mercilessly, treating him with contempt (verse 7). They taunt him about his faith (verse 8). All this was to be the experience of the Lord Jesus many years later (Matthew 27:39–44; Mark 15:31–32; Luke 23:35).

Lord, come to my rescue

Again he finds comfort in looking back over God's past record of faithfulness. From the moment of David's birth, God had been involved in his life (verses 9–10). Now he turns from the past to prayer. He asks God to continue to be with him, especially through this difficult time. If God does not stand by him, there will be no-one else who will do so (verse 11).

David's enemies must have made a concerted effort to bring him down. He certainly believes they would be satisfied with nothing less than his complete destruction. They were like 'snorting bulls' or 'roaring lions' waiting for the moment when they could either pull him apart or tear him to pieces (verses 13–14).

A side effect of all this stress was that David was extremely unwell. The description he gives of his symptoms indicates that he was struck down with a very serious complaint. His prospects for recovery did not look good. In addition to this these terrible people were trying to 'finish him off' by stabbing his hands and feet. We can understand why he was at such a low ebb (verses 14–17).

To add insult to injury, these enemies were attempting to degrade the psalmist by snatching his clothing from him, literally leaving him naked to face the world (verse 18). He turns to God in prayer. He asks God to intervene and save his life (verses 19–21). He tells the Lord that if he will act on his behalf, then David will speak to others on God's behalf. He will give public testimony to the greatness and goodness of God in his life (verses 22–28).

The psalm ends with the recognition that death must come to each individual, even kings. But the future will not be left without a generation which can speak for God (verses 29–31).

Questions

1. Have you sometimes felt that God had abandoned you? Why did you feel that? How did you react and what did you learn?

2. Our worship services often emphasize victory and triumph. Where does this leave people who are feeling abandoned by God? How can the church help them through this time?

3. When we feel as David did here, how should we handle these feelings when we are among non-Christian friends and colleagues? Hide them because they would be a bad witness? Or be honest about them? Why?

Crucifixion

John Stott writes: '. . . the sufferer's agony in Psalm 22:14–17 – his disjointed bones, his thirst and his pierced hands and feet – is a remarkable description of the horrors of crucifixion'.

Crucifixion was a cruel and slow death first developed as a means of execution by the Phoenicians. Later it was adopted by the Romans. The victim was nailed to a wooden crossbeam. The nails were driven through the wrists rather than the hands, because soft tissue of the hands tended to tear. The crossbeam was then hoisted by a series of pulleys and secured on to a vertical stake. The victim's feet were nailed to this stake.

The manner of death was slow, sometimes taking a number of days. It was also extremely painful. In order to breathe the victim had to pull himself up on the nails through his wrists and push down on the nails through his feet. This was, obviously, excruciatingly painful and extremely exhausting. In the end the person could not continue this process and so gave up. He would then suffocate.

The similarities between what David experienced and what the Lord Jesus was to endure at the time of his crucifixion, are too detailed to be ignored. Our Lord actually quoted from this psalm while he was on the cross (verse 1 and Mark 15:34). The mockery the psalmist experienced is paralleled in the treatment Jesus received from the priests (verses 7–8; see Matthew 27:39–44; Mark 15:31–32; Luke 23:35). Like David, the Lord Jesus was further humiliated by the confiscation of his clothing (verse 17 and John 19:23, 24).

Psalm 23

The Lord is my Shepherd

The Lord is our loving Shepherd, providing for us and leading us.

 This is probably the best-known psalm in the whole collection. It is frequently chosen to be sung at weddings and funerals. But to restrict its use to these occasions would be wrong. It is a psalm for the whole of life.

This psalm has caused writers down the years to struggle for suitable words to describe this wonderful song. Henry Ward Beecher called it 'the nightingale of the Psalms'. Charles Spurgeon referred to it as 'David's heavenly pastoral' and 'the pearl of Psalms'. This psalm has also been the subject of many well-loved songs and hymns, such as 'The Lord's my Shepherd' and 'The King of Love my Shepherd is'.

In traditional Jewish families this psalm is used as a 'grace' before meals.

The setting for the first part of this psalm is the countryside (verses 1–4). David grew up in a rural community and he uses a number of word pictures which are drawn directly from this background.

The shepherd and his sheep

The psalm begins with a bold claim (verse 1). David declares that the most powerful person in the universe (the Lord) is also his personal pastor ('my shepherd'). There is little doubt that he knew the Lord as his Saviour before knowing him as his Shepherd. This must be the pattern for all of us.

Having been a shepherd himself he understands that the sheep were his total responsibility. He had to supply all their needs. David is confident that with God as his shepherd he will lack for nothing (verse 1).

An earthly shepherd would lead his flock in rich pasture-land where they could both rest and feed (verse 2). God also meets his people's need for rest and refreshment (Numbers 10:33). In our lives, which are so often filled with stress and fatigue, sometimes we have to ignore our 'hurry up culture' and allow God to make us lie down and rest for a while. It is in these moments of quietness that we can read God's Word and reflect upon what he is trying to say to us. The Lord Jesus promised that if we are hungry for God we will be filled (Matthew 5:6).

It was common knowledge among shepherds that sheep need gently flowing water if they are to drink in safety (verse 2). Sheep are prone to breathing water into their lungs if the current is too swift and the water too turbulent. In this way they are susceptible to pneumonia. There is also the danger that if the stream is flowing quickly the sheep might fall in and drown. They have been known to die of thirst right next to a stream which is too fast flowing for their taste.

David believes that God will provide the appropriate place to find refreshment for his soul. He knows that with the Lord no believer need ever go thirsty (John 4:14; 7:37).

The sheep always need careful attention. They constantly require the shepherd to 'restore' them (verse 3). The word 'restore' can mean:

▶ To repair – to put back into original condition

▶ To refill – something that has been emptied

▶ To replace – something in its proper position.

All three meanings apply to the shepherd's work. Sheep need to have their fleeces rid of briars and parasites. When they are hungry (empty) they need to be fed, and when they wander off, as they often do, they need to be brought back to the flock. David sees this as a picture of the ongoing 'restoring' work of God in our lives.

Protection in times of danger

Sheep tend to wander off the right path if left to their own devices. David recognizes that we all tend to be a bit like sheep in this respect. That is why we need God's help to point us in the right direction. His own reputation rests on his right leading (verse 3, 'for his name's sake').

The shepherd is never more needed than in times of danger for the sheep. Sometimes the flock had to travel through deep ravines where there was little light. In those shadowy places the sheep had to rely on their shepherd to take care of them. He had to keep a constant watch for predators that might come out of the shadows and snatch one of the flock. In the event of an attack the shepherd would use his rod (or club) to drive off the attacker. He would then use his staff (shepherd's crook) to bring the sheep back into an orderly group again (verse 4).

For the believer there are periods in our lives when we have to walk through very dark times. What David refers to here is 'the valley of deep darkness', rather than the 'valley of the shadow of death'. The comfort for those who trust in God during these testing days is that they have the promise of his presence (verse 4, 'you are with me'). He knows that with God close at hand there was no need to be afraid. That is true for all of us. G. Campbell Morgan, commenting on this verse, noted that when we are assured of the Lord's presence 'this cancels fear'.

From the fields to the feast

In the last part of the psalm the scene changes from the open field to the banqueting hall (verse 5). David pictures God's people no longer as sheep but as guests at a grand reception. Here there is a victory celebration where the vanquished enemies can only stand and watch the victors enjoying their sumptuous feast (verse 5). The guests are all greeted with the customary 'anointing' of their heads with fragrant oil. The wine is flowing freely, no-one is going without. For Christians this banquet speaks of a day when we will all take our place at the 'marriage supper of the Lamb' (Revelation 19:6–7).

The psalm ends with a bold statement of faith. David has confidence that God will be with him throughout his time on earth. At the conclusion of his earthly life there will be a place for him in God's house for ever (John 14:1–3).

Questions

1. In what ways are you like a sheep? How have you been aware lately of the Lord acting as your shepherd?
2. We are not just individual sheep, but a flock. In what ways can you see the Lord 'shepherding' the Christian community to which you belong?
3. Those who do not follow the shepherd go astray (see Isaiah 53:6). What are the consequences of this? How do you see it being worked out in society around you?

The Good Shepherd

In the Old Testament God is seen as the Great Shepherd of his people (see, for example, Isaiah 40:11). F. B. Meyer commenting on this verse writes:

> Do not be afraid of God. He has a shepherd heart and skill. He will not over-drive. When he leads out his own sheep, he will certainly go before them, and they shall follow him. He suits his pace to theirs. Words can never tell his tender considerateness. If the way lies over difficult and stony roads, it is because there is no other route of reaching the rich meadow lands beyond. When strength fails, he will carry you. When heavy demands are made, he will be gentleness itself. He is the good Shepherd, He knows his sheep.
>
> (*Christ in Isaiah* (Lakeland paperbacks, 1970))

In the New Testament Jesus takes upon himself the title of Shepherd (John 10:1–18; 1 Peter 5:4). He is the caring and conscientious shepherd. Not only will he take care of us and feed us on his word, but he showed his willingness to lay down his life for those he loves.

When it comes to facing the future we can have great confidence in Jesus, the Great Shepherd of our souls.

Psalm 24

A song of praise and a prayer for purity

Everything and everyone in this world belongs to God. To enter into his presence we need to be clean from the inside out. We need to receive him as our Glorious King.

Psalm 24 is the third in a group of three psalms written by King David (Psalms 22–24). It seems to have been composed to commemorate his triumphant return to Jerusalem after recapturing the Ark of God (2 Samuel 6). Some years later this psalm was used to remember and re-enact a time of national triumph during temple worship. Pilgrims making their way to Jerusalem would sing words taken from the opening verses of Psalm 24.

God unlimited

Their song begins with praise to God because of his unlimited power and unlimited possessions. He owns everything and everyone. To realize this is to recognize that this world is not ours but God's. We are tenants not owners. Margaret Thatcher was correct when she said 'no generation has a freehold on the earth, all we have is a lifetime tenancy'. Not only does the earth belong to God because he created it (Genesis 1:1), but we, too, belong to him because he created us (Genesis 1:26–27). This means that no-one is on earth by accident, we are all part of God's plan and purpose.

God's approachability

David encourages us to think of God as unlimited, but we are not to think of him as unapproachable (verses 3–6). At first sight, however, these verses seem to indicate that entry into his presence is almost impossible. He appears to want to keep his distance from us. Even the use of the word 'hill' (verse 3) seems to give the impression that God is too high up for us to reach. Elsewhere God is depicted as appearing on the tops of mountains accompanied by thunder and lightning and the people are told to keep their distance or risk certain death (Exodus 19:12, 13: Hebrews 12:18–21). That is hardly putting out the welcome mat!

But if we accept all that the Bible has to teach us about God's character we will discover that God is far from unapproachable. He wants our friendship but he wants us to approach him on his terms not ours (see Hebrews 12:28).

The issue of how we are to approach God is now explored in detail. This is done through a series of questions and answers (verses 3–6). Probably the choirs outside the temple gates were to sing the questions and the choirs inside the temple area were to sing back the answers. It was all intended to be very dramatic, visual and highly symbolic. So the question was posed, 'Who can approach a Holy God?' The response came back, 'only those who have clean hands (that is outward purity . . . lives in relation to other people) and a pure heart (that is 'inner purity' . . . in relation to a Holy God). The strong implication here is that you cannot have the one without the other. David then goes on to show how this clean and pure life works its way out in practical terms. The person who wishes to approach the true God will have no time for any false deity. Naturally in these circumstances any hint of dishonesty would be out of the question (verse 4, see also Psalm 15).

This kind of life is bound to evoke a blessing from God and it does (verse 5). We must not imagine, however, that the psalmist is suggesting that this life which is blessed by God can be achieved simply by pulling ourselves up by our moral boot-straps. Far from it. The psalmist makes it very clear that to live such a life is possible only when we have God as our Saviour (verse 5). When this is the case, we also discover that our lives have been cleaned up from the inside out. There are no longer any charges against us, we are vindicated (verse 5) and we are free to approach God. These blessings of free access into the presence of a Holy God are available to each new generation which seeks his face (verse 6).

The King of Glory

The last section of this psalm (verses 7–10) celebrates the triumphant entry of the 'King of Glory'. Originally these words were probably written to greet King David when he arrived at Jerusalem. But they came to take on a far deeper meaning, referring not to an earthly king, but a Heavenly One.

When this King of Glory arrives he dwarfs everything. The gates are too small for him to pass through and so must be lifted up and out of his way (verse 7). When Psalm 24 was used in worship, choirs outside the temple gates would be requesting entry for the Glorious King. The choirs waiting inside would respond by asking for further details about this wonderful visitor. This dramatic method helped to heighten the expectation of the congregation as they awaited the imminent arrival of the King of Glory.

Questions

1. Why do you think that purity of 'hands and heart' is so important as we seek to approach God, to come into his presence?

2. How can we welcome the King of Glory into our local church (see Revelation 3:20)? What sometimes keeps him out?

3. 'The earth is the LORD's' (verse 1). What does this mean for the environmental issues we face today? How should it affect our own lifestyles as Christians?

Psalm 25

Teach me how to live O Lord

We need to ask the Lord to show us how to live.

Most of us need some help in memorizing words worth remembering. Here David uses a literary device – the acrostic – to aid the learning process. This is a form of poetry where each line begins with a letter of the alphabet, in this case the Hebrew alphabet (the exception is verse 22). We have already met this in Psalms 9–10.

Here we find David in prayer. It is worth noting how many of the psalms are prayers in musical form. There is a place for singing our requests to God as well as saying them.

Total dependence

David begins by making a statement of intent. He is going to commit his 'whole self' (his soul) to God in total dependence (trust). He recognizes that he has nowhere else to go, there is nothing else he can do and no-one else he can turn to. His only hope is God (verses 1–2).

We do not know the exact situation David was facing, but we do know that it was extremely difficult. If it was not resolved it would result in a victory for his enemies. If this were to happen David would be utterly humiliated (verse 2). In these dire circumstances he cries out to God for help.

In his prayer he reminds God (or is he reminding himself?), that in the past God has always proved to be trustworthy. History has proved that no-one who placed his or her hope in God has been let down. However, past experience had also proved to David that those who deliberately betray their friends are left without any valid excuse in their defence (verse 3).

Guidance through prayer

With the confidence that comes from proving God in the past, he now turns to consider future events. David believes that God has a plan for his life. He also believes that it is by way of prayer that this plan is revealed. He is not looking for a theoretical discussion about the different techniques of finding God's will. He simply wants to be open and teachable. It seems that God is only ever able to guide those who come to him with an open mind and a willing spirit (Psalm 32:8–9). In seeking to discover what God wants him to do, David is not attempting to limit God to one option. He is asking the Lord to show him how to live a life which is characterized by making the right choices (verses 4–5).

Guidance is not about adherence to a set of rules and regulations. It is all about a close relationship with God. A desire always to please the Lord in everything we do will result in us making sound decisions!

While in God's holy presence David suddenly becomes aware of just how sinful he is. Isaiah had a similar experience (Isaiah 6:1–6). David recalls with shame some of the activities of his youth which he knows must have displeased the Lord (verse 7). The lesson to learn here is that when we have sinned, it is not time that heals the heart, but God's forgiving grace.

David asks God not only to forgive his past sinfulness but also to put it out of his mind. He is confident that God will do what is right as far as his past is concerned.

This confidence comes from his belief that God always does the right thing because he is 'good and upright' (verse 8).

Picking up the theme of guidance again, David emphasizes the need for sincere humility on our part (verse 9). Those who humbly follow God will discover that he is both loving and loyal (verse 10). When we come into the presence of God it is quite common for the blinding light of his purity to reveal the dark shadows of impurity in our lives. David was very conscious that in comparison with God's perfection, he was far from perfect. He does not wallow in his past sinfulness, however, but asks God to forgive him (verse 11).

He now asks a question that has a direct bearing on the subject of guidance (verse 12). The point is clear: only those who have a deep respect for God can expect to be guided by him. Following his ways will lead to a rewarding life (verse 13). The greatest reward of all will be that those who know the Lord will be privileged to share the knowledge of his future plans. They will become his close friends and confidants (verse 14).

Closeness in prayer

To stay in such a close relationship we have to be in constant communication with God. We have to keep our focus always on the Lord to ensure that we are remaining in the centre of his will (verse 15).

As the psalm concludes David returns again to his troubled circumstances (verses 16–21). He asks the Lord to look straight at him so that during this difficult time he can see his face and know what he wants him to do (verse 16). The picture here is of a child looking at its parent's face to find approval or disapproval concerning a choice of action. Whatever happens he knows where his support lies. He is determined to place all his hope in the Lord (verse 21).

After praying for himself, David's vision widens to all the people of God. He not only seeks to be rescued himself but he also longs for all the faithful to be saved from their troubles (verse 22).

Questions

1. How do you approach the question of God's guidance? Do you expect specific instructions on things like whether to move to that town or whether to take this job? What do you learn from this psalm about the way God guides us?
2. What decisions are currently facing your church? How do you think you should corporately seek God's guidance?
3. How valid are these sources? How would you witness to someone who felt insecure about the future?

Psalm 26

Prepare me for your presence Lord

We need to be prepared to meet the Lord.

In the next three psalms the focus is on 'meeting with God' (Psalms 26, 27 and 28). In Psalm 26 David is asking God to ensure that he is in a fit state spiritually to enter his presence and worship.

He begins by asking the Lord to make it known to everyone that he has led a life of integrity (verse 1). The phrase 'blameless life' has here the sense of 'whole heartedness' and 'sincerity' rather than sinless perfection.

He has thrown his whole weight of trust on the Lord. This has kept him from falling flat on his face ('without wavering' means literally 'without slipping'). In other words he has proved that the steady path in life is to be found by completely trusting in the Lord (verse 1).

David now throws open the door of his life to God. He offers God free access to the secret places of his heart and mind (verse 2). He feels that he has nothing to hide and that the heavenly investigation will reveal nothing terrible. His confidence is based not on his own righteousness but on his right relationship to God. He has adhered to God's ways and has stayed close to the one he loves (verse 3).

Love God, hate evil

David's strong love for God results in his equally strong hatred of anything which was evil. Love for God and dislike of those things which are wrong are two sides of the same coin (verses 4–5). He will not even associate with those who deliberately flouted the law of the Lord (Psalm 1). This did not mean that he has a 'holier than thou' approach. He knew that he as much as anyone else needed to be 'clean' in order to come into God's presence (verse 6, see also Psalms 15 and 24). This idea of 'washing off the dirt of sin' before being involved in worship may come from a practice carried out in the tabernacle. Before a priest could enter the sanctuary he was required to wash his hands and feet. Presumably this was a symbolic gesture which indicated a cleansing from sin (see Exodus 30:17–21 and 40:30–32).

True joy follows true forgiveness

There is now a startling contrast to the sombre reflection on the need for forgiveness that was required before David could enter the presence of God. He bursts into loud praise telling all those who were gathered about the wonderful works of God (verse 7). A moment's consideration confirms that the pattern seen here is the pattern for all of us. We cannot find true joy in God's presence until we have found forgiveness for our sins. It is the most natural thing in the world to want to be with the one you love. David simply wants to be with the Lord all the time. He wants to experience God's special presence – 'His glory' (verse 8).

In the last section of this psalm he pleads with God not to sweep him away with the tidal wave of judgment that is to overwhelm those who are dispassionately involved in cruelty and corruption (verses 9–10). Rather he seeks God's help to live a life that would gain heaven's approval. He wants to experience God's salvation and mercy, not his judgment (verse 11). From this position of being accepted by God he looks forward to worshipping his Lord with the other gathered people of God (verse 12).

Questions

1. How do we prepare to 'meet with the Lord' in our personal prayer times and in our church services?
2. In what sense is the church the dwelling place of the glory of God (see verse 8)? How do Christians experience that glory there? How does the world outside seek it there?
3. Read verses 4–5. What do you think David means? How does it tie up with Jesus being the 'friend of sinners'? You might find 1 Corinthians 5:9–11 helpful.

The tabernacle

Verse 6 may contain a reference to the tabernacle. The tabernacle was also called the 'Tent of Meeting'. Originally it was a movable tent which provided a provisional meeting place for God and his people before the larger tabernacle was built. It contained the 'Ark of the Covenant' and other significant symbols of Israel's faith. The original tabernacle was pitched outside the Israelites' camp and Moses would go there to meet with the Lord. When the larger version was established it was erected in the middle of the camp signifying the presence of God in the middle of his people (see Exodus 25–27; 33:7–11; 35–36; 40:34–35).

In the New Testament the Greek equivalent of the word tabernacle is used to describe Jesus' earthly ministry (see John 1:14 where it is related to the word translated 'made his dwelling'). He brought with him the presence of God into the centre of humanity.

In verse 8 the word 'glory' translates the Hebrew word *shekinah*. It was used of the 'overwhelming presence' of God (see Exodus 33:12–23; 40:34–35; 2 Chronicles 7:1–3).

Psalm 27

Lord, I just want to be near you

In this psalm we express our pleasure at being in the presence of God.

In Psalm 26 David had considered how to prepare to enter into the presence of God. In Psalm 27 he thinks about the pleasure he will experience as he draws near to God.

The Lord of light

The psalm opens with a declaration about the salvation which David enjoyed. The Lord had illuminated his life and brought him into a saving relationship with himself (verse 1). He knew that there is no 'dark side' to the character of God (James 1:17). The light of God dispels all darkness. This is a theme which the New Testament writers pick up and apply to the Lord Jesus (see John 1:4; 9:5; 2 Corinthians 4:6). When the pathway of life is illuminated by the Lord of Light there is no need to be afraid.

Even when he was surrounded by vicious enemies who were trying to bring him down, David refused to give in to fear. He had proved that God was all the protection he needed. Those who sought to hurt him would, in the final analysis, only end up hurting themselves (verses 1–2).

The Lord is my stronghold

As a soldier he often pictured the events of his life in military terms. He imagines himself as a besieged city with all the difficulties that would entail. The scene here is not just a city under siege but an all out war. Even when David's life was like a nation under sustained attack his trust in God would not be shaken (verse 3). This confident stance did not come from his belief in his own ability but his knowledge that God was on his side (1 Samuel 23:26–29; 2 Kings 6:15–17; Exodus 14:19–20; 15:18–21; Genesis 12:2–3).

The Lord of beauty

All the difficulties that David ever had to face paled into insignificance in comparison to the one passion in his life, that of being close to God. He wanted to live as close as possible to the Lord he loved. He was totally preoccupied with God. Nothing else really mattered to him. David Livingstone, the great missionary explorer, had much the same attitude. He wrote, 'I place no value on anything I possess, except in relation to the Kingdom of God'. In the same way as he did for Livingstone, the Lord filled the whole of David's vision. Just as people in love want to gaze continuously at their beloved, so the psalmist wanted to 'gaze upon the loveliness of the Lord'. He was committed to pursuing the closest possible relationship to God (verse 4). True worship, according to David Owen, is looking upon God, concentrating our whole being – minds, eyes, ears, emotions and will – upon his presence, thereby offering him our best and laying ourselves open to his transforming grace (2 Corinthians 3:18). That is what the psalmist was seeking.

The Lord of protection

Although David is passionate about the Lord, he is nevertheless a realist about life. He knows that not every day will be filled with unbroken sunshine. The life of faith does have its downs as well as its ups. Even in the most difficult circumstances, however, when everything appears to be going wrong, he believes that his relationship with God will sustain him. He is assured that he will enjoy both God's presence and his protection. His security will be rock solid. He is certain that in the end he will triumph. Following his God-given victory over his enemies he will return to the Lord with grateful praise (verses 5–6).

David now turns to prayer (verse 7). The thrust of his prayer is for a deepening sense of the presence of God. He is not prepared to walk at a distance from God (verse 8). He cannot cope with the idea that the Lord might withdraw his presence from him ('forsake him', verse 9). The psalmist speaks confidently to himself thereby gaining assurance that God, who is a perfect parent, would never abandon his child (verse 10). In the end he has no other option than to depend totally on God for direction and protection (verses 11–12).

The psalm concludes with a statement of David's confidence. He believes that God will not withhold any good thing from him in this life. All he has to do is be patient and strong in his resolve to let God do his will in his way (verses 13–14).

Questions

━━━━━━━━━━━━━━━━━━━━━━━━━━━━━━━━━

1. What is the main desire of your life (see Matthew 6:21)? How far do you share David's longings expressed here?
2. Read verses 4–5. How far do you share David's feelings about meeting with the Lord and his people in worship? Why?
3. When you look at society around us, how do you think we should balance 'waiting for the Lord' (verse 14) with working to extend God's Kingdom?

Psalm 28

In your presence Lord my prayers are answered

━━━━━━━━━━━━━━

In a desperate time we can ask God for his help. Our prayer will be answered.

━━━━━━━━━━━━━━━━━━━━━━━━━━━━━━━━━

This is the third in a group of psalms which focus on the theme 'the presence of God' (Psalms 26, 27 and 28). Here David is facing a time of desperate illness. He feels that he might even die! His mention of the word 'pit' indicates that he fears not death itself, but that he might be unfairly assigned a place among those who are under the judgment of God.

A cry for help

In his despair he turns to God, the One in whom he can find stability ('O LORD my Rock', verse 1). He asks the Lord not to ignore his prayer ('turn a deaf ear', verse 1), especially at this time of great need. This prayer is really more a cry for help. In it David spells out his total dependence by lifting up his hands to the Lord, a common posture in prayer. The psalmist demonstrates by this action that he is coming 'empty handed' to God. He recognizes that he can do nothing himself to rectify the situation (verses 1–2).

It is quite clear that he wants to distance himself from those who deliberately disobey God. For these are the people who are out to deceive by their smooth talk. To associate with them would mean suffering the same fate. He has no intention of being among their number when God carries out his judgment (verses 3–5).

A cry of praise

From the idea of punishment he moves on to praise (verse 6). He thanks God for his ongoing patience with him. He takes comfort in the thought that his cry for mercy has been heard in heaven. Not only is God not going to punish him, he is willing to protect him. This is a source of great joy to him. His heart is almost bursting as he considers the wonderful love of God. He cannot refrain from singing a song of exuberant thanks and praise (verse 7).

The wonderful resources of God are not for David alone. They are available to all who place their trust in him. The psalm closes with a prayer that God's strength might be experienced by all his people (verses 8–9).

Questions

1. How easy do we find it to recognize our total dependence on God in times of trouble? For instance in times of illness how readily do we turn to the 'Great Physician' as well as to human doctors (see James 5:13–20)?
2. 'Raising hands' in prayer is biblical (see 1 Timothy 2:8). How

acceptable is it in your church? Why does it arouse strong feelings?

3. Read verses 3–5. In what ways do you see the same sins in our society? Where do they lead?

Psalm 29

Lord of Nature

We stand in awe of God's frightening power.

Thunderstorms are among nature's most awesome displays of power. The huge electrical discharge which results in the fireworks display in the skies is spectacular and sometimes frightening.

God's powerful voice

It may be that David was out in open country when he was caught in a ferocious storm. His thoughts did not turn to fear, however, but to faith. He looked beyond the mighty power of the thunderstorm and saw it as an illustration of the incredible power of God.

We should not think that David literally believed that thunder is God speaking. He simply saw it as a picture of the power of God's voice. The phrase 'the voice of the LORD' occurs seven times in this psalm. Some commentators think that this looks back to the creation story when God formed the universe and everything in it by the power of his words (see Genesis 1).

The psalm begins with David encouraging all the angels of

heaven ('mighty ones') to worship God for his glory and strength (verse 1). He believes that God is worthy of praise, not just because of what he has done, but because of what he is like. He deserves our praise because he is holy (verse 2).

God's power in action

The rest of the psalm illustrates this holy God's awesome power by a description of the movement of the storm from the far north of Palestine (Lebanon and Sirion, that is Mount Hermon, are in the north, verse 6) as it travels down toward the south of the country (the Desert of Kadesh is in the south, verse 8).

The flashes of lightning and the great claps of thunder speak to him of the power and majesty of God's voice (verses 3–4). The storm's intensity is seen in that it can break trees as if they were matchsticks (verse 5). Both the high ground (the mountains) and the low lands (the deserts) are affected by this earth-shaking storm (verses 6–8).

Even the trusty oak tree cannot withstand such an onslaught and lays twisted on the ground like a discarded piece of paper. The forests are no match for this storm, they are simply flattened. This power that David observes in the natural world causes his mind to focus on the supernatural world. He believes that the only response to God's power is to join with others to sing out a song of glory to God (verse 9).

God's power enthroned

In contrast to all that is happening on earth because of the storm, David pictures God sitting enthroned above it all. He is the One in ultimate control, nature is his tool and not his master. The psalmist knows that if God has enough power to control the elements, then he has power enough to spare. The wonderful thing is that he is prepared to share this power with his people. When we have assurance of, and abundant supply of, God's power we can experience his gift of peace (verses 10–11).

Questions

1. How does David's view of God compare with yours? Do you need to become more aware of the awesomeness of God's power?
2. Sometimes church worship can so focus on the mightiness of God as to make him seem far removed from us. Sometimes our worship can be so informal that we lose sight of this awesomeness. How can we find the right balance?
3. How can we help our friends who don't know God to hear 'the voice of the LORD' in creation?

Psalm 30

From sorrow to joy

When God is introduced into the picture sorrow turns into joy.

We do not know exactly what the title to this psalm means. It could be a special song which David composed to celebrate the dedication of the temple, the house of God. Such a song may well have been sung at the dedication of the temple which Solomon, David's son, was to build (1 Chronicles 21:18–26; 1 Kings 8:22–66). The Hebrew word translated 'temple' can also mean 'palace' (see NIV footnote). If this is the case the psalm would be expressing the joy David experienced at the dedication of his own palace (2 Samuel 5:11).

It seems strange that the title apparently has little to do with what the psalm is actually about. However, one thread does link the title with the rest of the song. It is a psalm that traces David's journey from deepest gloom to the most exuberant joy.

Gratitude

The psalm begins with David rejoicing in the Lord. He is so very grateful to God because he has rescued him from what must have been terrible circumstances. Whatever he had experienced, whether it was a physical illness or perhaps some malady of the mind, it felt as if he was at the bottom of some dark pit. The word 'lifted' (verse 1) literally refers to a 'bucket being drawn up out of a well'. But that experience is now in the past. He has been lifted out of the darkness into the sunlight. He knows that all the praise for this should go to God (verses 2–3).

Celebration

He then bursts into a song of praise. He is not satisfied with singing alone, either. This rescue had been so great that David wants everyone to share in the celebration (verse 4). The dynamo for such joy is the psalmist's experience of the patience of God. He knows that the Lord has every right to get angry with his people. Sometimes he does, but this does not last for long. David has proved that tears do not have to be the long-term experience of God's people. Just as night gives way to the first light of dawn, so too will sad times give way to times of great joy (verses 5–6; see also 2 Corinthians 4:17; John 16:20–22).

For a moment the psalmist turns from the theme of joy to reflect upon the time when he foolishly began to trust in himself rather than in God. He recounts how this was a very bitter experience. But he did not remain trapped in this way of living. When he realized his mistake he turned to God in prayer (verses 6–10). This soon led to a time of praise!

This psalm concludes with David in festive mood. He is so full of joy that it affects his feet! He cannot keep himself from dancing (see 2 Samuel 6:9). He feels as if God has removed the

111

trappings of the funeral. In those days people wore sackloth when mourning the death of a loved one. This has been replaced with the party clothes of joy. He wants to dance and sing in praise of what God has done. He would like this celebration to go on for ever (verses 11–12; see also 2 Samuel 6:5).

Questions

1. Think of a time when you were in the 'depths'. How did the Lord lift you up? How did you feel?
2. Why don't we dance in church very often? Do you think we should? Why or why not?
3. People around us seek happiness but are often very unhappy. How can we encourage them to cry to the Lord (verse 8) and let him lift them up?

Dance

An examination of the musical instruments in the Old Testament reveals that there was an abundance of percussive instruments (2 Samuel 6:5; Psalm 150). From this E. W. Eaton has concluded that 'a great deal of Hebrew music, both religious and popular, was dance music'.

There are a variety of Hebrew words which are translated as 'dance'. Among these are the Hebrew words meaning 'to skip', 'to twist and turn' and 'to dance and sing'. When David danced before the Lord, the Hebrew word used to describe his actions is 'to move around' (2 Samuel 6:14). We do not know what these ancient dances looked like. The form does not really matter. What is important is that the people of God recognized that movement as well as music was appropriate in worship (Exodus 32:19; Judges 21:23; 1 Samuel 18:6; Psalms 149:3; 150:4).

As Roger Forster once said, 'Dance is simply saying Hallelujah with your feet'.

Sackcloth

'Sackcloth' (verse 11) was a coarse material woven from either goats' hair or camels' hair. To put on sackcloth was a sign of sorrow and mourning (Genesis 37:34; 2 Samuel 3:31; 21:10; 1 Kings 21:27; 2 Kings 6:30; 19:1, 2; 1 Chronicles 21:16; Nehemiah 9:1; Esther 4:1–4; Job 16:15; Psalm 35:13; Psalm 69:11; Lamentations 2:10). It also symbolized repentance (Jonah 3:5, 6, 8) or humiliation (1 Kings 20:31, 32). It was accompanied by prayer and fasting (Isaiah 58:5; Daniel 9:3). To take it off was to indicate joy and relief (Psalm 30:11).

Psalm 31

Safe in your hands

There are no other viable options but to place our trust in the Lord.

This psalm was intended to reflect the theme of joy, to celebrate the fact that God had always taken care of his people during difficult times. In this there is a strong link with the previous psalm.

God is our refuge

The psalm begins with the writer thinking back over his life. He has proved that in the past God had not let him down. Now he is asking God to be with him through a trying time in his life. He wants him to be his security, to be his rock and his strong fortress. He needs God to guide him through tricky paths, where many traps have been laid. He has no other options but to hand his life completely over to God. This was a time when he had literally to 'let go and let God' (verses 1–5).

David knew the futility of turning to a 'false god'. He had observed those who had pinned their hopes on idols and he had not been impressed. As far as he was concerned there was no other route to take. He was committed to a life of trust in God (verse 6).

At a time when he was in deep distress God had not stood by detached and uninvolved. He had been right there at David's side and for this David was eternally grateful (verses 7–8).

God is trustworthy

We are not sure if, at this point in the psalm, the writer is still reflecting back on past experience or if some new tragedy had hit his life. Whatever the case it is the record of a deeply stressful time (verses 9–13). The point is that, through it all, David found that his trust in and dependence on God deepened. The Lord became more precious and more personal to him (verse 14). He also discovered that the events of his life were all under God's control (verse 15). With the assurance of the Lord's presence and the promise of his protection David was confident that even in the most frightening circumstances he would be safe (verses 16–22).

The psalm ends with David encouraging the people of God to love him more and to find their strength in him (verses 23–24).

Questions

1. In what ways has your trust in the Lord been put to the test? What was your experience of God at that time?
2. What evidence is there in your local church that people trust in God and love him passionately? How can we encourage one another to be strong and take heart (see Psalm 31:14, 23)?
3. Sometimes we must feel cut off from God's sight (verse 22). What can we do to help Christians who are experiencing distress? Think of specific people and situations you know.

That special moment

In verse 15 we have the phrase 'My times are in your hands'. G. A. Knight writes:

> The reference is not to clock time, but to those special moments in life when something memorable happens – marriage, birth of a baby, falling ill, recovering, a sudden awareness of beauty, of hearing 'the lost chord' – moments of deep meaning that never return, but which one can never forget. These all come from God; they are moments of *eternity breaking into time*. And the profoundest of these are those moments when one becomes vividly aware that God's face is shining on his servant. Awareness of that wonder drives out all the sense of horror at what the wicked one can do to one.
>
> (*Psalms*, Vol. I, p. 152)

Psalm 32

Forgiven!

Hiding sin only leads to greater hurt.

Many people believe that the background to this psalm is the dreadful episode between David and Bathsheba (read 2 Samuel 11). This may or may not be the case. What we  can be certain of is that the writer had done something which he knew really displeased the Lord. He was vividly aware that his conduct had erected a barrier between himself and God. This was causing him intense spiritual pain because he hated to hurt the Lord. In the light of this he did what we all must do when we recognize we have grieved the Lord. He said sorry. The effect was immediate. The relationship was instantly restored and the joy which had been absent returned.

This song springs out of a reconciliation between David and God. Appropriately it begins with a blessing. This sense of being blessed is the direct result of experiencing forgiveness. David rejoices in the fact that his past sins have been dealt with.

Notice the words David uses to describe both his sin and the method that God uses to deal with them. He speaks about his 'transgressions'. To trangress is to 'step over the mark'. It is, for example, to see a sign which reads 'keep off the grass' and then deliberately to walk on it. The psalmist also speaks of 'sins'.

This means 'to miss the mark', 'to fail to attain the standard' or 'to deliberately omit to do something'.

He refers to the person 'in whose spirit is no deceit'. The word 'deceit' literally means 'perverse' or 'twisted'. It indicates someone with a corrupted nature (verses 1–2).

Having given a detailed description of his sin, David now shows how God has brought about forgiveness in his life. The Hebrew word translated 'forgiveness' means 'to remove or to lift'. One aspect of receiving the forgiveness of God is to have the burden of sin lifted off us. He also talks in terms of having his sins 'covered'. This literally means that God puts our sins 'out of his sight'. Lastly David speaks about the Lord not 'counting' our sin against us. This suggests that the debt we owe God has been freely cancelled (verses 1–2).

Don't wait to put things right

The quickest and most sensible way to deal with sin is to confess it to God right way. The longer we try to hide what we have done the harder life becomes. David knew from personal experience that to try and hide sin leads to a great deal of hurt. Physically, emotionally and spiritually, unconfessed sin takes an awful toll on us (verses 3–4; see also Proverbs 28:13; 1 John 1:8–9). When we confess, however, forgiveness is sure to follow (verse 5). This confession and repenting of known sin sometimes has to be part of an ongoing process. For as Gordon MacDonald notes, 'every day with fresh brokenness we have to go back to recognize that the same evil that betrayed us before may betray us tomorrow in a different way'.

David now turns to the subjects of 'prayer' and 'guidance'. Both of these are affected by unconfessed sin. It is not until we put things right with God that we can really communicate with him, or he with us.

David encourages all who love the Lord to speak to him when things are difficult, to turn toward him in prayer and to find that he is the source of tremendous security.

117

God's way

God is willing not only to protect us, but also to show us the right path to take. Here he is described as a tender parent who carefully watches the first faltering steps of their child. In the life of faith, guidance is simply a matter of staying close to our heavenly Father (verse 8). The only requirement on our part is to be willing to go God's way. To ask for God's guidance and then to refuse to do what he says is the height of foolishness. The best route for us to take is the one which God has himself endorsed. When we do this we will discover his 'unfailing love' surrounding us (verses 8–10).

The psalm that began with a blessing ends in rejoicing. A song is never far from the lips of those who have experienced the forgiveness of God (verse 11).

Questions

1. Why do we tend to try to cover up our sins? Why is it foolish to do so?
2. How can we ensure that our church is a safe place in which to confess our sins?
3. The world around us sees the church as more concerned with sexual sins than with other kinds. Why is this? What other sins in our society should we be highlighting? How can we do this?

Psalm 33

Let's just praise the Lord!

This psalm shows us where true security is to be found.

There is no title for this psalm. The anonymous writer, however, was obviously full of joy when he put pen to paper. This song continues the theme of praise, following on nicely from the last verse of the previous psalm (Psalm 32:11).

Come on, let's celebrate

The psalm begins with an invitation to join the writer in a time of joyous praise and worship. This is a fitting task for all those who love the Lord. We should all want to celebrate who God is and what God has done. But the music is not limited to the sounds of human voices. Other instruments are brought in to help. The skilful playing of stringed instruments is accompanied by exuberant shouts of joy. There was nothing quiet or inhibited about this time of praise (verses 1–3).

Trust in God's word

The writer then gives the reasons behind this outburst of praise. He is rejoicing because he has confidence in the Word of the

Lord. He knows God's word can be trusted because God can be trusted. Anything that God is involved in has the ring of truth about it. He loves those things that are right and fair and wants the whole world to experience his unfailing love (verses 4–5).

People can trust in God's word because it is reliable. They can be confident in it because it is powerful. With words alone God was able to create the heavens and the earth (including the seas). In the light of this powerful creativity of God humankind can make only one response – reverently bowing in worship (verses 6–9).

God can also bring things to a grinding halt by words alone. His words are so powerful that even international statesmen cannot resist them. If he decides that the strategy of a certain country will not succeed, it will not succeed. His plans, however, no-one can stop (verses 10–11). God is able to decide the outcome of a nation's destiny. In the light of this it makes perfect sense to trust in him rather than in huge stock-piles of weapons. This is the best way to ensure national and international security (verses 12–19). The psalmist testifies that he and his people are determined to look to the Lord for protection. Real joy results from trusting totally in God (verses 20–21).

The writer began with praise and ends with prayer. He asks that God's unfailing love might be an ever-present part of his experience (verse 22).

Questions

1. How does your trust in God's word compare with the psalmist's? Why do we sometimes hesitate to trust it?
2. When we meet together to worship, how do our reasons for praise compare with the psalmist's? What can we learn from him?
3. What needs to happen for our nation to be 'blessed' (verse 12)? Is this a realistic hope in our multi-faith and secular society? Why or why not? Is it possible for a modern 'multi-faith' nation to say 'In God we trust'?

The harp

The 'harp' and the 'ten stringed lyre' (verse 2) are probably examples of an instrument known as a *kinnor*, the first musical instrument mentioned in the Bible (Genesis 4:21). It is thought to have been Syrian in origin and came in several varieties and sizes. It was made of different types of wood and could be played using a plectrum. There are Egyptian tomb paintings depicting this method. It was also played by plucking the strings with the fingers (1 Samuel 16:23). Some scholars say it had ten strings, others that it had eight. Whatever form it took, it was an instrument favoured by David himself (2 Samuel 6:5).

Psalm 34

Let me tell you what the Lord has done for me!

How can we keep quiet about all the good things the Lord has done for us? If God can do these things for us he can do them for others too!

It seems as if David cannot stop telling others about what the Lord has done for him. He just wants to keep on sharing with everyone the good news of the greatness of God. Indeed he wants to go further and boldly brag about the Lord (verses 1–2).

This desire to praise God all the time is not something that he wants to do alone. He welcomes others to join with him in glorifying and uplifting the name of the Lord (verse 3).

Now he begins to tell those who are prepared to listen the reasons for his praiseful attitude. He loves the Lord because, at a time when he was engulfed by the most terrifying feelings, God came to his rescue (verse 4). He continues by telling us how he had cried out to God in prayer and how the Lord had answered him. Part of God's answer was to send a heavenly protection service to ensure his safety (verses 5–7).

The psalmist calls for a response. He has told the audience how good God is, and now it is time for them to experience him for themselves. If they will take this step of faith they will discover that God will provide for their needs. They will never go without anything that is really worth having (verses 8–10).

In case those who are listening to him are still not convinced, David asks them to come a little closer to ensure a good hearing. If they take heed of his words he will teach them how to respect God as he does. Living a life which demonstrates reverence for him involves having respect for other people. The psalmist recognizes that this means that truth and honesty are always at a premium (verses 11–14).

It has been the writer's experience that God is on the side of those who do what is right and against those who continually choose to do what is wrong. It's as uncomplicated as that (verses 15–16).

The prayers of those who seek to honour God are always heard in heaven. More than this, they are assured of a more intimate experience of God when they are going through times of heartbreak (verses 17–18).

David knows that to live for God does not ensure a trouble-free life. Far from it! However, when something goes wrong in the life of a child of God all heaven is mobilized to mount a rescue plan (verses 19–21).

Questions

1. How readily do you tell others what God has done for you? If you find it difficult, why is this?
2. How good an advertisement is the church for Jesus? Does it make people want to run to him or run away from him? In what ways? How can we better draw people to him?
3. What groups of people are 'broken hearted and crushed in Spirit' in our society (see verse 18)? How could we bring them close to the Lord, offering practical help in their distress?

Psalm 35

Everybody is against me Lord!

Sometimes we have feelings of deep anger about our enemies.

Sometimes the Psalms can come as a shock to us as Christians, for some of them seem to be so hard and so ruthless. In them there does not appear to be any evidence of the 'spirit of Jesus', when he encouraged his followers not to seek revenge (Matthew 5:39). This particular psalm looks as if it fits this category well. But perhaps we are judging the psalmist who wrote this song too harshly. The psalms were written out of real situations and to express real feelings. We have to confess that sometimes the feelings that we have about people who treat us badly are less than charitable! What we have here

123

is David honestly expressing what he really feels in the presence of God. There is nothing wrong with that. Pouring out our true feelings to God may well act as a safety valve which can prevent an emotional or physical explosion.

Fighting on our behalf

There is little doubt that at the time of writing this psalm David felt under acute pressure. He feels that he is being overwhelmed by the continuous onslaught of his enemies. In fact, he believes that his very life is in danger. He is going through 'a soul-shattering experience' (G. A. F. Knight, *The Psalms*, Vol. I, p. 167). In this pressure cooker of stress he turns to God for help. We would expect him to do that. What we do not expect him to do is to pray that God might attack his enemies, which is what he does (verses 1–3). In Spurgeon's words he asks God to 'contend with his contenders' (*The Treasury of David*, Vol. I, p. 155). Literally he asks the Lord to go into battle on his behalf. According to Artur Weiser (*The Psalms*, p. 302), David uses 'the metaphorical language of war which is probably borrowed from an ancient tradition' (see Exodus 15:3; Psalms 24:8).

David wants his enemies' plans to boomerang back on themselves. He prays that the result will be that they, and not he, will end up defeated and disgraced. Following close on this request is his petition to God to literally blow his enemies away: to treat them as insignificant pieces of straw driven along by the wind. He asks that his opponents might stumble and fall, that their way would be made dark and their path slippery (verses 5–6). Spurgeon comments that for the enemies of God's people there was to be 'No light, no foothold, and a fierce avenger at their heels'.

In verse seven David uses the illustration of the hunter capturing an animal with a net hidden in a pit (see Psalms 7:15; 9:15). These enemies were like ruthless big-game hunters and David was their quarry! Without God's intervention he would be hunted down and mercilessly killed (verses 4–8). If this reversal of fortunes takes place this will bring him great joy (verses 9–10).

David has endured false accusations and a constant bombardment of innuendoes and vicious rumours which he believes he does not deserve. Has he not taken the troubles of these former friends upon himself? When one of these people lost a friend did David not mourn for him as a son would at the death of a mother? Despite this, when he found himself in trouble his enemies' only response was to laugh at him. Some went so far as to try and physically harm him (verse 16).

This was all becoming too much for David. As far as he was concerned it was way past the time when God should intervene on his behalf. If God was to step in and save David he would not be slow to tell everybody about it (verse 18).

David returns to the theme of being under pressure. He asks that God might save him from defeat, if only to prevent his enemies using his downfall as extra ammunition against him (verse 19). He again tells the Lord about the 'smear campaign' that he was having to endure. These accusations have no truth in them, surely the Lord knows this to be true (verse 25)?

Again he asks God to ensure that the enemies' tactics rebound on themselves (verse 26). Finally David prays that those who stand with him as his allies might also be able to join with him in a whole-hearted song of praise to God (verses 27–28). Artur Weiser captures the spirit of these verses when he writes, David 'counts himself among those who gratefully recognize that they are called to sing all the day long the praise of the majesty and righteousness of God' (*The Psalms*, p. 304).

Questions

___

1. How do you react when those you have tried to help turn around and try to hurt you? Why is it better to bring the injustice to God than to retaliate?

2. How honest and open do people in your church feel able to

be when they are angry or distressed? How can we encourage this openness in our groups and relationships?

3. Is there a place for outbursts of anger by Christians against the evils in the world? How can we channel this anger constructively?

Psalm 36

The burden of the Lord

When we come close to God we begin to feel how he feels when people reject him.

Sometimes when we get really close to God we become aware of what used to be called 'the sinfulness of sin'. The young prophet Isaiah had this experience when he encountered God in the temple. He discovered just how holy the Lord was and just how sinful both he and his people were (Isaiah 6:1–7).

Quality time with God

We get the impression that David had spent a prolonged period in the presence of God before he wrote this psalm. During this time he had managed to grasp something of what was going on inside the great heart of God. His burden had become David's burden. Now he had something to say that was straight from God. He was literally speaking God's words and expressing God's feelings (this is one meaning of the word oracle (verse 1; see also Amos 2:11).

No time for God

David had begun to realize some of what God felt about the utter wickedness of rebellious humankind. They have no respect for the Lord, no fear of him who can send them to hell or to heaven (verse 1). These people who have no time for God are victims of their own self-deceit. They have no concept of being sinners, even though their lifestyle demonstrates clearly that they are. It is obvious to him that these people are walking at a distance from God. They lie and cheat and dream up all manner of evil schemes. When it comes to choosing between right and wrong they make the wrong choice every time. They are locked into a life of sin. The ironic thing is that they cannot see this for themselves (verses 2–4).

God's unfailing love

The situation seems to be hopeless and would be so if it were not for the marvellous love of God. The extent of his love and righteousness no-one can measure. It can reach up to the highest part of heaven and it can reach down to a sinner in the lowest place on earth. The psalmist rejoices in the fact that all who turn to God will discover not only his love but also real life. The really sad thing is that David knows that some will be exposed to this love and this life and still choose to reject it (verses 5–12).

Questions

1. To be a servant of the Lord (see the title) we sometimes have to 'bear his burdens'. How can we come to sense what God was feeling about his church and his world?
2. To what extent is your church in touch with the sinfulness of life around it? How should we respond to it?

3. The world often sees the church as a middle-class establishment. How do verses 7–8 speak to this? What more can we do to demonstrate that God's love is for all groups in society?

Psalm 37

Don't wrestle just nestle!

We are encouraged to trust in God and not to envy the ways of the world.

The Dutch saint Corrie ten Boom's favourite saying was 'don't wrestle just nestle'! When we are close to God, nestling in his love, we don't have to wrestle with unresolvable issues. We can simply trust our Heavenly Father to do the right thing.

Don't be envious

In this psalm David offers similar advice. He tells his listeners not to 'fret' about, or be 'envious' of, those who choose to do wrong. The Hebrew word translated 'do not fret' is an interesting one. It literally means 'do not get heated' (see Proverbs 24:19). C. H. Spurgeon wrote that 'To fret is to worry, to have heart-burn, to fume, to become vexed'. We could express it as 'don't get all steamed up!'

The reason why some of David's listeners were getting themselves 'over heated' was that they were jealous of those in society who were doing the wrong thing but making a good living at it. To see someone totally ignoring God, and prospering in spite of it, is always difficult for a believer to take (see

Psalm 73). David understood why people felt this way. They were taking a short-sighted view of things. These people who apparently were so prosperous now have a very uncertain future (verses 1–2).

The psalmist believes that the right focus is upon the Lord, not upon the apparent success of those whose destiny is doubtful. He encourages believers to place the full weight of their confidence in God. For in trusting in him they will discover that he can provide all that they need for health, wealth and safety (verse 3).

This loving dependence upon God leads to a deepening relationship with him. The godly life is not simply a matter of gritting our teeth and putting up with it. It becomes a friendship which brings joy and delight. The result of this intimate relationship is that we end up wanting the very things that God wants. In this way he can give us a blank cheque, as it were. We can fill in the amounts and the things to be purchased because the Lord knows that his desires are our desires (verse 4).

Give it all to God

When we are really close to someone and really trust him or her it is not long before we begin to share our concerns with that person. The psalmist says that God wants to be that kind of friend. He wants believers to unburden themselves in his presence. The word 'commit' (verse 5) literally means to 'roll a burden or weight on to something or somebody else' (Joshua 5:9; Proverbs 16:3; 22:8). David encourages those who feel that they are carrying the weight of the world upon their shoulders to roll that burden on to the Lord (1 Peter 5:7). If they do this they will find that he will give them a glowing recommendation (verses 5–6).

It is always hard to be patient, but part of the life of faith is being willing to let God do his will in his time. Trusting in him involves waiting patiently for him to resolve issues that we cannot deal with ourselves. If we refuse to let God work it out and try to change things ourselves, this often results in frustration and anger. The psalmist warns against this approach. It is often when we are angry that we make the wrong decisions. Later we may wish that we had waited and been less hasty. In the end the situations which have caused us so much grief will look very different in the light of eternity (verses 7–15).

Heaven's perspective

Heaven has such a different perspective on wealth. The Lord does not want his people to try to get rich by any means possible. As far as he is concerned it is better to have a little that is honestly gained, than a lot which is acquired by corrupt dealings (verse 16; see also 1 Timothy 6:17).

The psalmist repeats his assertion that to follow the ways of the world will only lead to disaster. In fact God's people should stand in stark contrast to society in general. If others are stealing by deliberately defaulting on their loans, then believers should be recognized for being both honest and generous (verses 17–21; see also 2 Corinthians 8–9).

David's confidence in God's ability to provide for all his needs comes shining through in this psalm. He believes that we do not have to scratch our way to the top in order to claw as many material possessions for ourselves as possible. This is not necessary for those who trust in God. They can rest in the certain knowledge that the Lord will meet their needs (verse 25; see also Philippians 4:12).

The psalmist returns to the short-term prospects of those who live their lives without any reference to God. He says that in contrast to those who scurry around attempting to provide for themselves by wicked means, believers should continue to trust in the Lord. In the end those who patiently wait for him to act will see that they have made the right choice (verses 27–38).

The only thing that really lasts is our relationship with God. David is confident that we can leave our security for this life and the next in his capable hands (verses 39–40; see also 2 Corinthians 4:16–18).

Questions

1. Do you tend to be jealous of those who break all the rules and yet still seem to succeed? How does this psalm help you to deal with those feelings?
2. What can you learn from this psalm about the right attitude to money? What are the implications for (a) your own finances (b) your church's finances?
3. What examples can you see in our society of 'the wicked' bringing down 'the poor and needy' (verse 14)? What can we do to bring 'righteousness' and 'justice' into these situations?

Psalm 38

I feel terrible Lord

Sometimes when we are in distress we see a connection between that distress and sin.

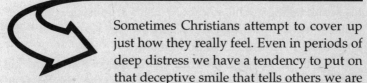

Sometimes Christians attempt to cover up just how they really feel. Even in periods of deep distress we have a tendency to put on that deceptive smile that tells others we are all right, when really we are not. Thankfully the psalmist did not go in for this kind of Christian cover up. He is quite prepared to tell us exactly how he feels, even when what he has to say is not very pleasant. The great thing about such honesty is that it helps others to be honest too. It enables them to admit they have a need and to find help to resolve their problem.

It is obvious that something had gone terribly wrong in David's life. This psalm describes a person who is in deep distress. We are not sure what exactly had happened to make David so upset, but it is clear that he blames himself for whatever had taken place.

Illness and punishment

The psalm reveals that the writer has become very ill indeed. This sickness he believes to be part of God's punishment for his sin. It is true that God can use sickness to teach us many valuable lessons. C. H. Spurgeon used to say that his congregation could learn more about faith from a period of illness than they could from listening to his sermons! It is not right, however, to conclude from this that every illness is given by God as a punishment for sin, or an opportunity to learn more about the Christian life! This would be to take a much too simplistic approach.

It may well be that David has become ill because of the guilt he is experiencing, and as a result of all the emotional trauma that he is going through. He certainly testifies to the fact that his guilt has become 'a weight' that he can no longer carry (verses 1–4).

Physically the psalmist is near to death. He talks of his pulse racing and his vision fading. Even his hearing is affected. He is in a very serious condition indeed (verses 8, 10, 13). Not only is his health failing but his so-called friends are deserting him and his enemies are plotting against him (verses 11–12, 16, 19–20). For David this is a very low point indeed.

In this time of terrible suffering David speaks to the Lord. He acknowledges that he can hide nothing from the One who can see the most hidden areas of every heart. Even the sighs of the depressed sufferer are known to God (verse 9). There is no use in pretending in the presence of the Lord. All the psalmist can do is honestly confess the sins that have been troubling him so greatly (verse 18).

The psalm ends with David asking God to stand by him. He wants the Lord to move rapidly to come to his aid (verses 21–22).

Questions

1. Have you ever linked 'sickness' to unconfessed sin? What obvious dangers are there in this approach?
2. What does your church teach about 'sickness' and 'healing'? How does it tie in with the lessons we learn from this psalm?
3. Sometimes Christians cover up their true feelings and problems because they don't want to be a 'bad witness'. Do you think it would be better to be as brutally open about them as David was? Why or why not?

Psalm 39

What's life all about Lord?

How can we make sense of life?

Through the years there have been many different responses to the question 'What is life all about?' William Shakespeare said that life 'is a tale told by an idiot, full of sound and fury, signifying nothing'. For the poet Henry Longfellow, life 'is but an empty dream'. These individuals seem to have had a very gloomy outlook on life.

If we are honest we have all had times when we have thought

the same thing. We have looked at the world in which we live and have asked ourselves 'What's it all about?'

Speak out or be silent?

In this psalm David is asking some searching questions about life and 'the meaning of it all'. He begins by being discouraged, not by what he sees in the world, but by what he sees in his own life. He finds it a constant battle to keep himself in check. He has to watch not only what he does but especially what he says (verse 1; see also James 3:1–12).

David is afraid to speak out about what is going on in the world. He feels it is likely that he will say the wrong thing. In spite of this he feels impelled to speak. The situation is too serious to remain silent. The acts of evil that he sees around him call for a response. It is as if he has a fire burning inside his heart. He must register his protest. Emperor Haile Selassie said that 'throughout history it has been the inaction of those who could have acted, the indifference of those who should have known better, the silence of the voice of justice when it mattered most, that has made it possible for evil to triumph'. There is a time when keeping silent is sinful (verses 2–3).

The meaning of life

As he begins to speak out about what he believes to be right he finds that it stirs within him some basic questions about the meaning of life itself. It is often the case that when we engage in debate with others it causes us to question what we really believe for ourselves.

David begins by asking God about the length of his life. How long will he live and will his life count for anything? It was the cartoon character, Garfield the cat, who said that he wanted 'to leave paw prints on the sands of time'. David wants to make an impact on human history. It is a goal all of us should have (verses 4–5).

He recognizes that gaining all the wealth in the world will not give him the sense of satisfaction he desires. In the end all the things acquired here on earth have to be left behind. The old saying is true, 'there are no pockets in shrouds'; you can't take wealth with you (verses 6, 11).

Making sense of it all

David concludes that there is no answer to the question, 'what is life all about?', if you leave God out of the picture! The late David Watson said that before he became a Christian he studied philosophy and natural sciences at Cambridge University, looking for the meaning of life. He later admitted that trying to find out what life is all about by studying philosophy is about as useful as looking for a black cat in a dark room. The psalmist can find no help in his search for meaning until he turns to God. Only God can deal with his real problem of sin. Only he can make sense out of life on earth.

David felt as though he was a foreigner living in unfriendly territory. If God would not be his friend who else would he have? He had no-one else to depend on except the Lord. There was no other person who could answer his disturbing questions about the meaning of life except God. He is left with no option other than to cling to God. In the end that is the only way to make sense of a sometimes senseless world (verses 7–13).

Questions

1. How can we decide when we should speak out and when we should keep quiet?
2. The church is often seen as irrelevant to real life. How can we ensure that our church helps people to make sense of their everyday lives?
3. Anger against injustice (verses 2–3) is one reason people sometimes give when asked why they entered politics. What

are the pros and cons of Christians getting involved in politics, whether at a local or national level?

Psalm 40

Patience rewarded

Do we want to be a 'willing slave' for the Lord?

It's hard to be patient when we are going through a particularly difficult experience. The temptation is to shout out to heaven, 'Lord get me out of this right now!'

Willing to let God take control

We do not know the historical background to this psalm or whether David had been suffering emotionally, physically or spiritually before he wrote it. What is clear is that he felt as if he had been at the bottom of a dark and muddy pit and that God had stepped in and lifted him out of those terrible circumstances. Now, instead of slipping and sliding around in that awful place, he is able to find a firm foothold. He uses word pictures to describe the Lord's deliverance. He is deeply grateful for God's intervention. He counts his blessings, remembering what God has done in the past. This is always a spiritual tonic (verses 1–2).

The marvellous rescue that God achieved is not to be kept a secret. If the Lord has been able to help David in this way, then he can help others too. He is filled with confidence that his testimony in song will cause others to want to know the Lord (verse 3). When we worship God for who he is and what he has done it acts as a tremendous witness to other people.

David continues with his declaration of belief and trust in God. He wants everyone to know that he is firmly convinced that there is only one God. The person who really wants to be blessed will worship the Lord alone (verse 4).

He now moves from witness to worship. He is overwhelmed by the goodness and greatness of God. The Lord has taken care of his past and is mapping out his future. Remaining in the will of God, however, is not a matter of fate. It is about having the right heart attitude and making a choice to serve God in all that we do.

A willing slave

David again uses word pictures to convey his meaning. He speaks of having his ears pierced. This was the sign of someone who was prepared to be a willing slave (Exodus 21:6). The psalmist knows that God wants more than external obedience (burnt offerings and sin offerings). He wants a desire to obey him which comes from the heart. The psalmist is willing to do what God wants because this is the burning desire of his heart. His one aim in life is to try to please God. Years later a greater Son of David would enter this world with the very same desire (verses 6–8; see also Hebrews 10:5).

Willing to proclaim God

David now turns to the task of proclaiming the good news about God. David is consistently ready to speak for his Lord (verses 9–10). He is not prepared to be a secret disciple, he always goes public when it comes to God's love and faithfulness to him. David is full of confidence that the God who took care of him in the past will take care of him in the future (verses 9–11).

Willing to trust God in our weakness

God is faithful but this does not mean that believers will live a trouble-free life. David knows this from personal experience! He tells the Lord that his life is so full of trouble that there are too many to count. David also recognizes that it is impossible to run away from sinful acts in the past. Eventually they catch up with you and overtake you. In the middle of this troubled and guilt-ridden time he finds that even his courage has deserted him (verse 12). At this point David cries out to God. He asks for God's immediate intervention on his behalf. He prays that those who were trying to bring him down might be brought down themselves in defeat and disgrace (verses 13–15).

David's prayer isn't just focused on his enemies' activities. He also remembers to pray for his friends. He asks that all those who seek the Lord's salvation might be rewarded by experiencing great joy and gladness in their lives. From then on their constant theme would be the 'Greatness of God' (verse 16).

In the final verse of this psalm David reflects on his own weakness and helplessness. But far from depressing him these thoughts encourage him! In his weakness he has learned how to really depend on the Lord (verse 17).

Questions

1. What motivates you to speak about Jesus to others? If we are reluctant to do so, why is this?
2. Why is 'going through the motions of religion' so unacceptable to God (see Mark 7:6–8).
3. What does it mean to have the 'Law written on our hearts' (see Jeremiah 31:33–34)? What difference should this make to our service for the Lord?

Psalm 41

Let it be Lord, let it be

We should want God's will to be done always. Part of this is to take care of the weak.

 We now come to the final song in the first section of the book of Psalms. The very first psalm began with a blessing (Psalm 1:1) and this psalm begins the same way (verse 1).

David knows that God has always been on the side of those who are least able to defend themselves. It is clear to him that a blessing awaits those who imitate the Lord in regard to his treatment of the weak (verse 1; see also Matthew 25:31–46; Luke 10:25–37).

God our healer

This blessing is seen in a number of promises that David sets out in this psalm. He believes that God will not only protect those who live according to his will, but he will also preserve them. When they are sick he will restore them to health (verses 2–3, Good News Bible). We know that God is able to heal those who are unwell. Often he uses the prayers of other believers, especially those who are called to be leaders in their local church (see James 5:13–16). But although we know God can heal, we also know he sometimes chooses not to. This is difficult to understand but we have to allow for his sovereign will in all things.

The psalmist claims for himself the promises he has just spoken of. Like all promises in the Bible they have to be personally appropriated. He specifically asks for God's help in dealing with past sin. He also prays for protection from the accusations and attacks of his enemies (verses 4–8).

It appears that David has been hurt by a close friend who has betrayed him. He asks for God's help and strength in order that he might get revenge on this person. We do not know if God answered this particular prayer. There are some prayers that God cannot always say yes to. What he is prepared to do is to help his servant live a life that is known for its integrity.

The psalm concludes with praise to the God whom history cannot contain and a prayer that his will might be done (verses 9–13).

Questions

1. How do we react when we are let down by a friend, especially if that friend is a Christian? How does this psalm help us to deal with our feelings of betrayal?

2. In what practical ways could your church demonstrate a 'regard for the weak' (verse 1)?

3. What can we learn from verses 5–9 about the evils of gossip? How should Christians deal with this issue when people try to gossip to us or about us?

Psalms 42 and 43

Depression

When we are suffering from deep depression we can bring our feelings into the presence of God.

Psalms 42 and 43 are thought to be two parts of the same psalm. This is why there is no title for Psalm 43.

One reason for writing a song is to tell others exactly how we feel. This two-part psalm falls into this category. It lets us know exactly what David was going through and how he felt about it. We find him in the grip of a dark bout of depression. The Christian psychiatrist, Louis McBurney writes,

Depression takes many different forms. Emotionally it appears as a feeling of sadness, not wanting to go on, hopelessness and, in extreme cases, self destruction. Physically it is expressed through tension, headaches, tiredness, bowel disturbances and chest pain, even though a physician would be hard pressed to find anything physiologically wrong. (*Leadership Magazine*, Spring Quarter, 1991)

It has been estimated that six times as many women suffer from depression as men, especially those with small children.

Depression is not an uncommon experience for believers either. There are several examples in the Bible of those who had to walk through what has been called 'the dark night of the soul'. Following his triumph on Mount Carmel Elijah was threatened by Queen Jezebel and ran away. Later he plunged into a deep depression (1 Kings 19). Jonah the prophet became severely depressed when his prediction of the imminent judgment of God was thwarted by the Ninevites' act of repentance (Jonah 4). John the Baptist became subject to depression after his imprisonment, even questioning whether his cousin Jesus really was the promised Messiah (Matthew 11:1–6). And from these psalms we know that David was not immune to this extremely trying experience either.

Throughout history there have been Christians who have been used greatly by God and yet have suffered terribly from 'dark moods'. One was William Cowper, who wrote many famous hymns in partnership with ex-slave-trader John Newton. C. H. Spurgeon, the famous Baptist preacher, confessed to having times when he was so down-hearted that he felt like quitting the ministry altogether.

True believers do go through times of deep emotional suffering. They need our loving prayer and support, not our criticism and suspicion.

Separation

To discover why David feels the way he does we need to ask where he is as he writes this song. It appears that he is away from home, but more importantly he is absent from the House of God. David describes his location as being in 'the land of Jordan, the heights of Hermon – from Mount Mizar' (Psalm 42:6). From his description he is residing in the northernmost part of Israel and is unable to get down south to Judah. He is experiencing a nasty bout of homesickness. Depression can be caused by not being able to be where we really want to be. David certainly feels cut off from the ones he loves.

He also feels spiritually isolated. Being in the far north he is unable to join with those with whom he usually meets to worship God. This leads David to enter a downward spiral of discouragement. He feels not only 'cut off' from God, he also feels forgotten by him as well (see Psalms 42:9; 43:2; 13:1).

Attack

His geographic location is not the only problem he is facing. He is under attack by his enemies. Their onslaught is causing him to feel completely oppressed. They are observing his suffering and then kicking him while he is down. These people's taunts feel to David like a severe blow to the ribs. They are that painful! What makes matters even worse is that his enemies are actually using as an accusation the very thing David is thinking, namely, where is 'God in all this?' (Psalms 42:3, 10 and 43:1).

Grief

The result of all this is that the psalmist is in a very bad way emotionally. He finds that he is crying all the time. He is living on a diet of tears rather than on truly nourishing food (Psalm 42:3). David is literally down in the dumps. He is utterly depressed by the whole situation (Psalm 42:5). He feels that life is simply too much for him and that any moment he will have a complete breakdown (Psalm 42:7).

Like so many who experience these dark times of depression, David is going through a grieving process. To him it feels like losing a loved one. A sense of profound loss seems often to accompany periods of depression (Psalm 43:2).

If we ask how David is getting on spiritually we may be shocked to discover that he is doing surprisingly well. He has managed to keep his spiritual passion throughout this terrible ordeal.

Survival

David turns to his experience of the wilderness to illustrate how he feels. To survive in the desert a deer must take in large quantities of water. In the same way David believes that to survive spiritually he must drink deeply from the waters of God's living presence. Even in this time of depression David has not lost his desire to meet with the Lord. He realizes that the only way out of his difficulty is to have an encounter with God (Psalm 42:1–2).

Cure

The way that he emerges from this period of depression is striking. He talks himself out of it in the presence of God. He asks himself a series of questions (Psalms 42:2, 5, 9, 11 and 43:2, 5). He interrogates himself to discover how he came to be in this condition.

Then he begins to prescribe for himself the method of treatment. He tells himself to think back, to reflect on the things he used to enjoy (verse 4). Counting our past blessings is often the route back to blessing in the present. C. H. Spurgeon affirms this: 'It is great wisdom to store up in the memory our choice occasions of converse with heaven – we may want them another day'.

After telling himself to look backwards, David tells himself to look forwards. Three times he tells himself that if he trusts in God he will emerge from this depression. It is as if he is saying to himself that 'God has come through for me before . . . he will come through for me again. I will survive this!' (Psalms 42:5, 11 and 43:11).

All this is not amateur psychology on his part. He does not believe that he can simply 'will' his way out of this depression. He is only too aware that 'prayer' has to be part of the answer. In the light of this he asks God to guide him back to himself, as he guided the people of Israel in times past (Psalm 43:3).

Recovery

Although David is not yet fully recovered emotionally, he looks forward to the time when he will join with others to give thanks to God for his goodness (Psalm 43:4). His faith is able to look beyond his present circumstances to see what God would do for him in the future. He is confident that a time is coming when this dark cloud will lift and he will again have a smile on his face. The Living Bible captures David's sentiments superbly in Psalm 43:5: 'Trust in God! I shall again praise Him for His wondrous help; He will make me smile again, for He is my God.'

Questions

1. What is your experience of depression, either in yourself or in a loved one? How would this psalm have helped?
2. How can your church help those who are emotionally unwell? How welcome do they feel? If you were depressed, would there be aspects of your church's services that would make you feel even worse?
3. What facilities are there in your area for mentally ill people (psychiatric units, hostels, day centres), and how adequately do they meet the need? How could your church get involved in this issue?

The Sons of Korah

There are twelve psalms that mention 'the sons of Korah' (Psalms 42–49, 84–85, 87–88). They are descended from the rebel leader of the same name. His children were spared when he died because of his rebellion (Numbers 26:10–11). One part of this family found employment as temple doorkeepers

(1 Chronicles 9:17–20). Another branch became singers and musicians in the temple choir (1 Chronicles 6:31, 33, 39, 44).

Psalm 44

Where have we gone wrong Lord?

Sometimes we feel abandoned by God, but do not believe that we have done anything to deserve this.

In this psalm the author is seeking to put into poetic form the corporate feelings of the people of Israel. They feel as if they have been abandoned by God. It could be that  this sense of abandonment is the result of a recent defeat that they have suffered in battle. Whatever the reason for their despondency, they all feel that God's absence was not justified.

Learning from the past

In a time when children were not packed off to school to get their education much of the teaching took place in the home. In Israel it was the responsibility of the father to instruct his children. Part of this education was to learn about the history of their people and this psalm was apparently used for this purpose.

This is no ordinary history lesson. These people have a special past to reflect upon – not because of what they have done, but because of God's involvement with them. It was he who defeated their enemies. It was he who established them in a prosperous land. A constant lesson for all new generations to learn is that it is God who is responsible for any positive achievement, not them (verses 1–8).

Coping with the present

It is always easy to look back on the past with rose tinted glasses. The present situation, with its harsh realities, is often more difficult to cope with. The people of God in this psalm are going through a particularly tough time. They feel humiliated by recent military defeats. They believe that they have become 'jokes' as far as some of their enemies are concerned. Defeat and derision have brought about a feeling of disgrace. As far as they are concerned, they have become an international laughing stock (verses 9–16).

What makes things even worse is that they cannot find any reason for receiving this kind of treatment from God. Have they forgotten to pray, have they been disloyal to God? Have they done anything that might have incurred God's displeasure? They do not believe that they have (verses 17–18).

The cost of serving God

In spite of their belief that they are innocent of any crime, they are experiencing the heavy weight of God's judgment upon them. Or so they believe. It could be that they are interpreting events incorrectly. This dark time of defeat and national bewilderment may not be the result of something that they have done wrong at all. Perhaps this difficulty was not because they are doing something wrong, but because they were doing something right. Derek Kidner could be correct when he says that, 'what Israel was suffering was a battle scar rather than a punishment'. There is always a cost in serving God. These wounds are the result of being involved in spiritual warfare.

This is certainly the way Paul interprets this passage in his letter to the Romans. He has no doubt that serving the cause of Christ would result in suffering and perhaps even death. The glorious truth that the apostle goes on to emphasize is that in all these things Christians can be victorious through trusting in Christ (verses 19–22; see also Romans 8:36–38).

In the New Testament when the disciples are afraid that they might drown, they shout for Jesus to get up from his sleep and save them (Mark 4:38). Here the same request is made of God. The Israelites urge God to stir himself and intervene on their behalf. The answer to their request, however, is already present in the words that they employ in their prayer. For they speak of God's 'unfailing love'. These words must act as a reminder that in the Lord's service, even if we have to suffer, we are never called to suffer alone (verses 23–26).

Questions

1. Do you sometimes misunderstand what God is doing in your life? How can this psalm help?
2. In this psalm the writers look back at how God had helped his people in the past. Why is this important? What part could your church's teaching programme play in this?
3. Why do Christians tend to get persecuted for living 'good' lives? Share your experiences.

Psalm 45

A wonderful wedding

A wedding celebration is a time for rejoicing.

 Sometimes authors experience what has been called 'writer's block'. This is when all inspiration dries up and the words simply refuse to come. The psalmist has no such problem here. His words seem to flow easily. The reason for his ability to write so effortlessly is the wonderful theme he has turned both his mind and his pen to. It seems that 'love' makes poets out of all of us. Another fine endorsement of romantic love is to be found in The Song of Songs.

The occasion for which this poem was composed was a royal wedding (see 1 Samuel 18:27; 1 Kings 16:31). It may be that it was intended to be read to the happy couple at an appropriate moment during the ceremony.

A handsome bridegroom

The psalmist begins by launching straight into a glowing description of the bridegroom. He is a king and of royal stature. This monarch stands head and shoulders above everyone else. His words are characterized by kindness, a grace given by God himself. When it comes to his military prowess there is no-one

149

in comparison. This king champions all that is right and true and always does what is best for everyone. Yet, even with these obvious skills and virtues he remains unaffected. There is not a sign of pride to be found in this individual (verses 2–5).

From praise of an earthly king the psalmist now turns to give glory to the Heavenly King. He describes God's rule as being never-ending in its scope or length (verse 6).

From heaven the poet turns his focus again to the earth. He praises the human king because of his godly approach to life. Like God, this king loves what is true and good and hates all that is false and evil. Because of this the Lord has blessed the king with all manner of riches. His clothes have about them the aroma of the most expensive perfumes and his home is decorated to the highest standard. He even has the luxury of soothing music whenever he has need of it. This bridegroom is some catch indeed (verses 7–8)!

A beautiful bride

The bride's description is no less impressive. She is obviously extremely beautiful. The king is absolutely besotted with her and totally captured by her stunning good looks. Not only is he in love with this wonderful woman, but others are queuing up to shower her with gifts. The people around her, and the possessions she receives, are of the highest possible quality as befits a royal bride.

The psalmist believes that this woman lacks nothing, except perhaps a little wise advice. He encourages her to see this marriage as the beginning of a new relationship. Old family ties are no longer quite so important. The main focus of her life now is to be her husband (verses 9–14; see also Genesis 2:24).

Weddings are times of great happiness and this is no exception. The psalmist paints a word picture of the bridal party approaching the king's palace with great joy (verse 15).

Looking to the future the writer is convinced that the children that result from this union will be counted among the world's greatest citizens (verses 16–17).

Questions

---

1. Why do Christians sometimes think it's not very 'spiritual' to talk about romantic love? How does this psalm contradict that idea?
2. How does your church prepare couples for marriage? What improvements do you think could be made?
3. 'We don't need a piece of paper to live together in a committed relationship'. Why should couples bother with a marriage ceremony?

Biblical cosmetics

Oil of joy (verse 7) refers to perfume oil or cosmetic ointment (see Ruth 3:3; 2 Samuel 14:2).

Myrrh (verse 8) was obtained in biblical times from India, Arabia and Abyssinia. It was mixed with other ingredients to create a very expensive perfume, a luxury item (Song of Songs 1:13). It was a symbol of extravagance and beauty (Esther 2:12; Psalm 45:8; Proverbs 7:17; Song of Songs 3:6; 4:14; 5:13). In the New Testament it was one of the gifts presented to the infant Jesus (Matthew 2:11). It had other less pleasant uses. It was used in Jewish burial (John 19:39). Also, it was mingled with wine and used as a narcotic to relieve pain (see Mark 15:23).

Aloes (verse 8) is a general name for the aromatic wood of various plants. The only mention of the true aloe is found in John 19:39. Most of the biblical references are to 'eagle wood' or 'sandalwood'. This was imported to Egypt from India and Malaya and was valued as an ingredient for incense and perfume (Psalm 45:8; Proverbs 7:17).

Cassia (verse 8) is another name for the dried flowers of the cinnamon plant. It was mixed with myrrh, aloes and oil to create a perfumed ointment or sometimes anointing oil (Exodus 30:24).

Ivory (verse 8) in Hebrew is 'tooth' or 'tusk', hence elephant tusk. In the ancient world carved and unprocessed ivory was very expensive. It naturally became a token of wealth and luxury (Amos 6:4). It was also a valuable item to be traded (Ezekiel 27:15; Revelation 18:12).

Psalm 46

Let go and let God

When all around us is chaotic we can turn to God to find stability and peace.

Spurgeon called this psalm, 'the song of holy confidence'. He has not been alone in finding great strength in this psalm. The reformer Martin Luther, when he was going  through particularly difficult and dangerous times, would often read this psalm. Indeed, one of Luther's most famous hymns, 'A mighty fortress is our God', is based on Psalm 46.

God protects his city

The background to the writing of this psalm seems to be an unsuccessful attack on Jerusalem. The writer sees this as a direct intervention on the part of God to safeguard his city and his people.

Having seen God's saving intervention it is not surprising that the psalmist begins this song with a bold declaration of faith. He pictures the Lord in terms of an impenetrable city.

Those who 'live' under his protection have nothing to fear. God not only protects his people, he strengthens them as well. The psalmist has proved that God has all the strength he needs to face any situation. His strength is sufficient to deal with any eventuality.

Not only is God all powerful, he is also ever present. In times of trouble he is never an 'absentee parent'. When things get really tough the Lord can be counted upon to 'be there' for his children.

With this kind of confidence there is never any need to panic, no matter what the world might throw at us. Even when everything else around us appears to be crumbling in front of our eyes, we can still be secure. God is totally dependable and totally reliable. The world may fall apart but he will not (verses 1–3).

Any city that does not have a reliable water supply is at an extreme disadvantage when an opposing army lays siege to it. Without drinking water the battle would soon be lost. The city of Jerusalem had an adequate supply of water to meet all its citizens' needs. Indeed, it had such an abundant supply that it was a source of joy and delight for those who lived there.

God is with us

There is more to rejoice about in the city than simply the provision of good clean water to drink. God, himself, has chosen to live amongst his people in Jerusalem. His presence there ensures the city's ultimate protection against whatever chaotic events were taking place in the world outside its walls. As if to underline this growing confidence in God, the psalmist boldly asserts that he is utterly sure of his presence and protection (verses 4–7).

The writer now invites those listening to his song to come with him on a journey through history. He points out that God is the ultimate power in the universe. It is the Lord, not human beings, who ultimately decides the destiny of nations. It is God who brings about international peace, not diplomats and statesmen.

Then, right in the middle of this description of the turmoil of human history, God speaks directly through the psalmist to his people. The Lord says that in the chaos that often typifies our lives and our world we are to stop what we are doing, stand still and look at him. The Hebrew word translated 'be still' (verse 10), literally means 'cause to fall away, let go'. It is as if God is saying to us that we are to let go of our plans and trust him to do what is best. The really important thing is not squabbles between various people and nations. The crucial issue is that everyone should begin to recognize that all history is moving toward the day when God will be acknowledged as Lord over all the earth. This thought puts all our petty schemes into a different perspective (verses 8–10).

The momentous concept here is that this Almighty God is on our side! This is something we need to stop and think about quietly. The psalmist introduces a 'Selah' after each mention of the awesome power of God, so that we can reflect upon the implications of such a marvellous statement (verses 7, 10 and 11).

When the Methodist evangelist John Wesley was near to death he took comfort in the promise of God's presence found in this psalm. With his last breath he said 'The best of all is, God is with us.'

Questions

1. Think of a time when events shook your private world. How did you experience God's protection and strength?
2. Is your church a place where you find spiritual refreshment? How does this take place?
3. This psalm paints a picture of God as our refuge and fortress. How can we communicate our security in Jesus to a world full of insecurity?

Psalm 47

God is King

This psalm helps us to praise God, the Great King.

 Like many of the psalms this one can be understood at two levels. Firstly, it can be read in terms of the celebrations surrounding a royal enthronement. Interpreting the psalm in this way we understand that the writer is occupied with the splendour of the occasion and the greatness of the earthly king. It was never the author's intention, however, to limit his readers' vision to the confines of earth alone. He wants us to look beyond the earthly to see the heavenly. A greater King is being referred to here. Seen in this light, this little psalm takes on an even greater significance. The setting now is not the grandeur of some earthly monarch, as wonderful as that might be. The scene is one of all nations gathered to worship God!

Music in worship

Down the centuries all manner of different instruments have been used to accompany spiritual songs. Perhaps the most basic are our hands. But this is not a time just to give God a reverent, yet hearty, 'round of applause'. The music of countless human voices are to be employed as well. The task of worshipping God

155

is too vast to limit to a few people or a few instruments. The psalmist believes that all the nations of the world should join in this musical extravaganza to the glory of God.

The theme of this international anthem is the awesome greatness of God. He deserves such extravagant praise because of his past victories. Only he has been able to bring all the peoples of the earth to heel. Only the Lord has been strong enough to subdue all the world's would-be rebels (verses 1–3).

The psalmist marvels not only at God's greatness but also at his grace. It was undeserved love that God had showered upon his people. For this he should be given never ending praise (verse 4).

God is on his throne

The writer pictures the Lord taking his place on the throne, from which he will govern the universe with justice, wisdom and mercy. This is too great an event to keep silent. Trumpets, singers and others join in a triumphal shout of joyous worship. Everyone joins together to flood the heavens with sound. The King of Kings is worth singing and shouting about.

Then comes the declaration that God is King. He reigns over all people, everything belongs to him (verses 5–9). He is a Sovereign worthy of all our praise!

Questions

1. What are the things that you get excited about in your experience of God?
2. How important is music in worship? How could your church make better use of its musical talent?
3. If 'God reigns over the nations' (verse 8), why is there so much war and corrupt government in our world today?

Psalm 48

Location, location, location

The place where God dwells is beautiful and holy.

 The estate agents tell us there are three qualities that will make your property attractive to a potential buyer. They are 'Location, location, location!' People really do care where they live. The more striking the setting, the happier they are.

A beautiful city

In describing the city of God, Jerusalem, the psalmist asserts that its setting is absolutely perfect. This psalm sets out all the qualities of the city where God has chosen to make his presence felt in a special way.

The psalm begins with a declaration of the greatness of God. This is an important point. For it is not the city itself that is special, it is exceptional only because God is there. The author continues by assuring us that the Lord is worthy of our praise. He deserves all the adoration we might give him.

The writer is convinced that Jerusalem is the most beautiful place in the world. It stands above every other city in its lofty position. He does not mean it is the highest in metres above sea-level, but that spiritually it is the loftiest. The fact that Jerusalem

157

is God's city means that it is a joy not only to those who live there, but to all that live on the earth.

When this psalm was written it was a commonly held belief that there was a mountain in the north, the highest in the world, where all the gods lived. Verse 2's mention of the 'heights of Zaphon' refers to this. The psalmist has no doubt that, in comparison to Jerusalem, this mythical mountain was no more than a molehill. This is the author's estimation of the elevated stature of the city. He knows that there are cities built upon higher hills than the one upon which Jerusalem was placed. But those other cities were small in comparison. They all lacked the one factor which made Jerusalem great, the presence of the living God (verses 1–3).

An impenetrable city

Jerusalem is the target of many attacks. But, all those would-be invaders find to their great cost that the city has a defender who couldn't be beaten. The most sophisticated battle plans are nothing to him. The largest naval fleets are like toy boats on a pond as far as he is concerned. Using the wind as his weapon, the Lord shatters these mighty ocean-going ships as if they are made of matchwood (verses 4–7).

The psalmist does not want people to think that all this talk about Jerusalem is his own invention. Others can testify to the truth of what he has said.

A meeting place with God

From the city in general, the writer moves on to speak about a place in Jerusalem which has become special to himself and many others. This is a holy place where people can meet with God and take time to reflect upon their relationship with him. Here they can dwell on the fact that the Lord is the source of joy and gladness. Here they can marvel about just how big God is. His fame has spread throughout the earth (verses 9–11).

The psalm concludes with an invitation to go on a sightseeing tour of the city. The psalmist tells these tourists to take special note of all that Jerusalem has to offer. Its greatest attribute is that God has placed his stamp of ownership upon it (verses 12–14).

Questions

1. Do we need special places now where we can go to meet with God? Why or why not? Which are yours and why?
2. How can churches catch a vision of the greatness of the God who dwells in them?
3. What are we doing to spread God's praise to the ends of the earth (verse 10)?

Songs of Zion

The psalmist mentions 'Zion' three times (verses 2, 11 and 12). G. A. F. Knight has some helpful information about the development and use of this term. He writes,

At the north-east corner of the city there was the highest point, known as Mount Zion. The significance of the word Zion grew and developed over the centuries:
a) Zion was where the temple and royal palace stood, that is to say, on it was found the seat both of government and of divine worship.
b) Later on, Zion became a poetic name for the people of Israel themselves.
c) Still later, after they were driven from Jerusalem in 587 BC by the Babylonian conquerors, Zion came to be used of the whole people of God.

d) Sometimes the name was even used for the little local church building which one attended Sunday after Sunday.

e) But in church liturgy Zion came to be used as the name even of the heavenly city!

(G. A. F. Knight, *Psalms*, Vol. I)

Psalm 49

Winners and losers

It really matters what you invest your life in.

It is very easy to be short-sighted as far as this life is concerned. Millions of people live simply for today because they believe that this life is all there is. For these individuals  when death comes that is the end, there is nothing more to look forward to. As the atheistic philosopher Bertrand Russell put it, 'when you die you rot.'

Jesus did not follow this line of thought. He taught that there is more to human existence than the seventy or so years we have here on earth. In fact he warned his disciples against focusing exclusively on this world and forgetting that there is a world to come. The danger in this approach is that those who appear to be winners in this life can turn out to be losers in the next (see Mark 8:36–37; Luke 12:13–21).

The ultimate statistic

The shortness of life here on earth is the subject taken up by the psalmist. He believes that this issue is so important that the whole population of the world should take notice. The writer knows that death is the ultimate statistic – one out of one dies. Benjamin Franklin wrote that nothing is certain in this world except death and taxes. Everyone is affected, both rich and poor. There is no way to avoid this universal appointment that every one of us will have to keep (verses 1–2).

In the light of the serious nature of this subject, the psalmist has some words of wisdom for all those who are prepared to listen. His message is very clear. One human life is worth more than all the world's wealth. No amount of money can buy happiness here on earth, or ensure a place in heaven.

In the final analysis all the wealth gained in this life has to be left behind. This is why it is so futile to invest all your energy providing for this life and neglecting to make provision for the life to come. In the end only tombstones will be left as a memorial to those who placed their faith in material goods. By trusting in wealth they demonstrate that their real faith is in themselves and not in God.

A certain future

The future of those people who do not place their trust in God is clouded with uncertainty. For the believer, however, there is a relationship with God that goes beyond the grave. The psalmist is confident that he will see life after death (verses 14–15).

Those who live for now and ignore tomorrow will be the ultimate losers. They may receive applause here on earth but heaven remains unimpressed. Wealth may be able to buy friends on earth but it certainly cannot buy friendship with God.

The psalm ends on a very sober note. If a person lives only for themselves they are living less than fully human lives (verses 16–20).

Questions

---

1. What are you investing your life in (see Mark 8:36–37)?
2. When we spend so much money on church buildings are we not investing in this life rather than on the next? What should be the priorities for the church's finances?
3. What can we say to people who trust no-one but themselves? How can we show them the folly of this and point to an alternative way to live?

Psalm 50

Stop play acting

God is never content with an 'outward show of religion'. He wants to see reality.

David Watson said that, in Britain, the biggest road block to evangelism was the established church! When Christians say one thing and live another it can be most off-putting to the watching world. The charge of being hypocrites is a difficult one to live down (see Romans 2:17–29). This is why Jesus was so outspoken against those religious leaders of his day whom he considered to be playing at religion. What they said they believed did not seem to impact the way they behaved. For Jesus this was unacceptable (see Matthew 6:1–4; 23:1–37).

God the Father hates hypocrisy no less than does his Son. In this psalm he calls the people of Israel to meet with him to hear some very straight talk.

The psalm begins with a declaration of God as the 'Mighty One', the One who has the right to address the whole world. He has something very important to say and nothing will prevent him saying it. God is not happy with the conduct of his Covenant people. The community which is supposed to reflect his righteous character has gone sadly wrong (verses 1–6).

God the judge

The scene painted here is that of the court room. God is the judge and his people are in the dock. The Lord begins to lay out the charges that he is about to bring against them. It is not because they have failed to do all the right religious things that he is displeased. Rather, it is because they have gone through these rituals without their hearts being involved in the process.

God does not need to be supplied with meat, he has the whole animal kingdom at his disposal. That is not the point of the sacrificial system. The purpose of bringing sacrifices to God is to show that the individual has experienced a change of heart. This was the centre of God's dispute with Israel (verses 7–15).

Saying one thing, living another

They were doing all the appropriate religious practises. At the same time, however, they were in rebellion against God. The people of God were attending worship but they were not obeying his word. They all knew the commandments but made no effort to keep them. Indeed they blatantly broke them. They were saying their prayers, but with the very same mouths they were slandering other members of their own family. How could God's people begin to think that he would tolerate such a situation.

For a time God had remained silent in the hope that his people would change their ways. This only had the effect of convincing them that he did not mind their actions because he was of a similar character to them. Nothing could be further from the truth.

The time to keep quiet had gone. Now the Lord was going to sort this situation out face to face. He would make sure that these wayward individuals knew beyond a shadow of a doubt that he was very angry with them indeed.

The psalm ends with a grim warning. If they do not change their ways they will face destruction at the hand of God (verses 16–23).

This psalm stands as a stark reminder to all of us who claim to be believers. The really important question is not what kind of church we attend, but what kind of lives we lead. Are we reflecting in our lives what we say with our lips? If we are not then this psalm tells us to stop play acting!

Questions

1. Why was Jesus so hard on hypocrisy (see Matthew 6:1–4; 23:1–37)? How can we guard against it?
2. What becomes of the church when it is 'all form and no force' (see 2 Timothy 3:5; Mark 7:6)? How can we ensure it doesn't happen to our own church?
3. 'The church is full of hypocrites.' How can we share the gospel with people who think this?

Covenant

The concept of covenant goes back to the book of Genesis (see Genesis 15:7–20). There God entered into a covenant with Abram giving to him and his children territory which stretched from Egypt to the Euphrates. The Hebrew word is *Berith* meaning 'an agreement'. However when it comes to a covenant between God and man we are not dealing with two equal parties. God's covenant is essentially a matter of grace (undeserved love, Psalm 89:28). His covenant is always linked with his 'covenant love' (*hesed*) or 'mercy' (see Genesis 9:15; Jeremiah 33:20–22). The word 'everlasting' or 'eternal' is used of God's covenant in various places (see Leviticus 24:8; Deuteronomy 33:9; Jeremiah 33:21; Malachi 2:4).

Prelude to Psalm 51

Not perfect just forgiven

When we don't nip sin in the bud, it can end in catastrophe.

 It is sometimes difficult to find the historical setting for individual psalms. With this psalm there is no such difficulty. The title does not spare David's blushes. The sordid situation and David's full involvement in it are there in black and white for all to see.

The background to Psalm 51

To appreciate the full significance of the words of this psalm we need to look at the sorry story recorded for us in 2 Samuel 11. The very fact that this account is in the Bible should assure us that we can trust it to give us a reliable picture of human nature. It shows us that the greatest of God's leaders can fall into the grossest forms of sin. Matthew Henry wrote, 'The best of saints may be tempted to the worst of sins'.

David was no 'average' believer. He received the highest accolades from God himself. He was known as 'a man after God's own heart' (see Acts 13:22). Yet this man committed a terrible series of acts.

Was this sin a moment of madness on David's part, or was it something that had been waiting to happen? The Bible indicates that this event was not simply a spontaneous act but rather a result of David's incomplete surrender to God. For years he had allowed God to be Lord in every area of his life, except his sexuality. This was to be his Achilles' heel.

David the superstar

We know that David was a handsome man. The Bible tells us that he was 'ruddy, with a fine appearance and handsome features' (1 Samuel 16:12). Not to put too fine a point on it, he was a bit of a hunk! Good looks can put extra pressure on people. David was not only handsome, he was famous. The women of his day made up pop songs about him. These told of his exploits in battle (1 Samuel 18:6–7).

The king was attractive to members of the opposite sex, this is beyond dispute. What is also beyond doubt is that he enjoyed the company of beautiful women. Lots of them! Over a twenty-year period he had accumulated eight wives and many other women who served his sexual needs. This was in direct disobedience to God's Word. There are clear instructions to kings not to accumulate horses, riches and wives (Deuteronomy 17:16–17). The consequence of this disobedience was that this sin had been eating away at the fabric of his life.

All this kind of sin needs is the right opportunity. For David that opportunity was presented to him in the shape of another man's wife.

A slippery slope

When these events took place David was probably in his early fifties. Sexual sin is no respecter of age. It was the time of year when traditionally kings went to war. On this occasion David decided to stay at home. Was he simply tired of the battle or was he getting lazy (see 2 Samuel 11:1)? Whatever the reason for the king staying back at the palace, he had let his guard down and was open to a sucker punch (a punch landed when you aren't expecting it).

A clear downward moral pathway can be traced through this story. David was wandering around on the top of his house and he noticed from his vantage point a woman bathing. He could have simply turned away. But he chose not to do this and it was the beginning of his plunge towards committing adultery (see 2 Samuel 11:2). That pathway could have led to both his and Bathsheba's execution (Deuteronomy 22:22).

It all began in David's mind. What we think about affects the way we behave. If we dwell on impurity we will live impure lives.

After David looked at Bathsheba he began to lust after her. The king was the most powerful person in the land. What he wanted he could have. He abused this position of trust. He sent for the woman and she consented to have sexual intercourse with him. She had little choice (2 Samuel 11:3–4)!

The king might have thought that this night of passion was the end of the matter. He could not have been more wrong. A few months later Bathsheba sends David a message that makes his blood run cold. She is pregnant with his child.

At this point David, the brilliant soldier who is so cool under fire, panics. Instead of coming clean and confessing his sin to God he sends for Uriah, the husband of Bathsheba. He tries to get Uriah to sleep with his wife. If Uriah complied with the King's suggestion everyone would think that the child was his and not David's. But Uriah declares that that would not be appropriate when his colleagues are out in the battle field. Even after David gets him drunk, Uriah refuses to have intercourse with Bathsheba. David is in real trouble and he knows it (2 Samuel 11:4–13).

Now the plot thickens and David involves others in his treacherous actions. He sends a letter to General Joab telling him to arrange to have Uriah killed 'in the line of duty'. The ultimate irony for Uriah is that he plays postman for his own death warrant.

The dastardly scheme works and Uriah is killed. David's response on hearing the news of his death is sickeningly smug. Normally he would have been furious if a soldier had been killed through using such sloppy battle tactics. On this occasion he is relieved.

The king thought that the matter was resolved. He could now marry Bathsheba legitimately and they could live happily ever after. The whole 'Uriah' incident was now a national secret. However, a well kept secret on earth is an open secret in heaven. God knew exactly what David had done and he did not like it (2 Samuel 11:14–27).

A word from a prophet

A year later God sent the prophet Nathan to David (2 Samuel 12:1–15). Instead of telling the king the error of his ways in a direct way, Nathan chose to tell a parable. This was a simple story of a powerful farmer taking advantage of a powerless smallholder. The rich man took the little sheep that meant so much to the poor man. This was grossly unfair and David realized this. His response was that the rich man should die for his unkind actions.

David's reaction is surely the sign of a tender conscience. Like the rich farmer he had taken advantage of a person who was unable to defend himself. He had taken something very special from Uriah, the wife that he loved. Like the rich farmer he had shown no pity when he had Uriah deliberately killed. It hardly needed to be said, but Nathan said it anyway, 'You are the man' (2 Samuel 12:7).

Nathan continues by spelling out clearly the consequences of David's sin. Both he and his family would be affected by his wickedness (2 Samuel 12:7–12). Indeed until he makes his confession of sin David is himself still under the sentence of death (2 Samuel 12:13).

As we go on to study the psalm which details David's sorrow over his sin, we will become deeply aware of his true remorse over the things he did. We will see that sin does not just affect the person who commits it. Sometimes those who appear to be totally uninvolved are affected too (2 Samuel 12:13–20).

Psalm 51

Not perfect, just forgiven

We can ask God to forgive even our most terrible sins.

This psalm was written as David faced up to the terrible nature of his sin and the possibility of God's forgiveness. Someone has said that this psalm is a 'series of convulsive sobs wrung out of the heart of David'. We can well imagine the high tension and the deep emotions that must have surrounded the psalmist as he seeks to come clean with God (see Psalm 32:3–5).

Face sin honestly

He at once recognizes the seriousness of sin. David has rebelled against God. What he did was not just a disgrace on earth but an insult to heaven (verses 3–4). He turns to the Lord with a repentant heart. Truth and wisdom demand that we all turn from our sin and turn toward God to receive cleansing.

Repentance, however, is no easy option. It is not 'cheap grace' that we are dealing with here. Being repentant means that we are sorry enough not to do that particular thing again. It means making a clean and absolute break with the past (verse 6; see also John 8:1–11).

The king approaches God on the basis of his mercy and his unfailing love (verse 1). The word for mercy which David uses is interesting in this context. It implies that 'the one who asks for mercy has absolutely no right to receive it'. If mercy is granted it is undeserved. All a person can do is say, 'God, have mercy on me, a sinner (Luke 18:13).

David throws himself on the mercy of God. He relies on the fact that God does not treat us as our sins deserve (Psalm 103:10). The sins that David had committed, adultery and murder, were both capital offences (Exodus 21:12; Leviticus 20:10; Deuteronomy 22:22). Under sentence of death David asks for God's undeserved forgiveness and cleansing.

He understands that he has 'soiled' himself by his actions. He needs to have this filth wiped away. The language he uses describes a 'foul garment that needs washing'. He is quite aware that sin has been a real problem from the day he was born. It has managed to mess up his life in a variety of ways. The only answer is for God to deal with his sin by washing it clean away (verses 2–9).

Forgiveness is costly

This cleansing process is costly. In the Old Testament it involved animal sacrifice. In the New Testament we are told that our cleansing is at the cost of Jesus' life (1 Peter 1:9). Our forgiveness is free but it is hardly cheap!

David not only asks for cleansing, he also wants a completely fresh start. He asks God to give him a new heart which will beat in time to his own. The psalmist wants to know the refreshing of the Holy Spirit. This new touch of God, he believes, will bring about a new joy in his life.

When we experience reconciliation with God it is not long before we receive a recommissioning from God (John 21:15–25). David wants to get back to serving the Lord as quickly as possible. This work for God will call for great sacrifice. David has learned that true sacrificial living flows from a heart that is humble before God (verses 10–19).

Questions

1. If what we think about really does affect how we behave, how should this influence what we read, watch and listen to?
2. Is there enough teaching about 'sexuality' in the church? Would more teaching on this subject help or hinder? In what ways? How should it be done?
3. Why is it that a Christian leader who has had an affair rarely gets back into full-time ministry? In the light of Psalm 51:10–19 and John 21:15–25 is this really fair?

Cleansing from sin

The words which David chooses to describe his forgiveness are full of meaning. For instance the phrase 'blot out my transgressions' means to 'erase them so completely that no trace remains' (Exodus 32:32; Numbers 5:23; Colossians 2:14). The phrase 'Wash away all my iniquity and cleanse me from my sin' (verse 2) is a term applied to washing dirty clothing.

The words he uses to describe his sin are also significant. The three words he chooses are 'transgression', 'to overstep the mark', 'iniquity', 'to be morally corrupt' and 'sin', which means 'missing the mark, failing to reach the divine standard and goal' (verses 1–2).

In verse 5, he says he was 'sinful from the time my mother

171

conceived me'. J Oswald Sanders writes, 'David was not casting any reflection on his mother, or suggesting that conception is in itself sinful. Rather, he was indicating that he now saw that his outward crimes were only the expression of his inveterately sinful nature.'

In verse 7 David says 'Cleanse me with hyssop'. This refers to the cleansing of a leper (someone suffering from some form of skin disease). Part of this process was to dip a bunch of hyssop in a container filled with blood and then to sprinkle it over the leper seven times (see Leviticus 14:6–7). Alternatively it could refer to the process of decontamination of a person who had been in contact with a dead body (Numbers 19:16–19).

Psalm 52

Rotten to the core

It's hard to cope with people who sacrifice others in order to gain popularity for themselves.

The title of this psalm gives us its background. David had just experienced a painful parting from his closest friend Jonathan (see 1 Samuel 20:41–42). He had also discovered from Jonathan that Saul was still committed to ending his life (see 1 Samuel 20:12–13, 30–31 and 35–42).

The city of priests

Following this David went to a town called Nob. This was a place where many priests and their families lived (see 1 Samuel

21). Abimelech, who was one of the priests there, gave David and his men a place to rest and food to eat. The only bread available for them to eat was the special loaves which were normally offered to God as part of the worship service. The priest would allow him and his men to eat this bread only when he was assured that they were spiritually prepared to do so (1 Samuel 21:1–6).

A treacherous spy

All appeared to have gone smoothly. The band of outlaws was able to eat and gain strength. Unknown to David, however, a deadly problem was developing. One of Saul's men, Doeg, had remained in Nob. Outwardly he was there to worship God. Inwardly his thoughts were focused on betrayal not blessing. He saw this as an opportunity to hand David over to Saul. In this way he would gain privilege and prestige for himself (1 Samuel 22:7).

Betrayal

David's band of men left Nob and travelled to the Philistine city of Gath. Doeg, however, returned to report to his master all that he had seen and heard. He told Saul how the priests at Nob had aided and abetted the fugitive David (1 Samuel 22:9–10). Abimelech was sent for immediately. Even though he protested that he was only helping someone he considered to be a loyal servant of the king, he was sentenced to death with his entire family (1 Samuel 22:11–17).

The problem for Saul was that nobody wanted to carry out this gruesome task. Nobody that is, except the unscrupulous Doeg. He quickly dispatched the eighty priests, their families and all the other men, women and children of the town. Not even the animals were spared this bloody massacre (2 Samuel 22:17–19).

Only one person lived to tell the tale that day. His name was

Abiathar, Abimelech's son. He managed to escape and find his way to David to whom he reported all that had happened and Doeg's part in it.

David took the news very badly. He believed that his oversight was the direct cause of the tragedy. He knew that he should have realized that the treacherous Doeg would go straight to Saul. David blamed himself for the death of this young man's father. All he could do was to offer Abiathar a home and future protection (2 Samuel 22:20–23).

This whole sorry story weighed heavily upon David's heart and mind. Later, while reflecting back on this terrible atrocity, he penned this psalm (verses 1–9).

David has a very low opinion of Doeg, and who can blame him? He believes that Doeg brought about the murder of the citizens of Nob out of a sordid craving for personal fame. Doeg might have a reputation among his friends for being a 'hard man', but as far as God is concerned he is nothing more than a thug. In the Lord's sight this man is an utter disgrace.

This enemy of God and his people has a tongue that is a deadly weapon. His words to Saul result in hundreds of innocent people losing their lives. They are not only deadly, but are deceitful too. He could never be relied upon to tell the truth.

The honesty of the psalmist is striking here. He really wants this evil man to be severely dealt with by God. Gordon MacDonald says that 'evil must be named and sin must be hated'. David speaks of a sudden disaster striking Doeg's life. This catastrophe will come directly from heaven itself. It seems that some crimes are so terrible that only the Lord himself can deal with them (verses 1–4).

So complete will be Doeg's punishment that it will become the stuff of which stories are made. When people hear this terrible tale they will either quake with fear or shake with laughter. Whatever their response, they will all recognize that Doeg's downfall came about because he wanted glory for himself, rather than for God. There is no ultimate benefit from rising to the top when to get there you have stepped on the backs of others (verses 5–7).

For David there is only one option open to him. He will depend on the God who never fails. Other people might betray us but the Lord will never let us down. This dependability calls for a response from his people (verses 8–9).

Questions

1. David felt guilty about what had happened to the priests at Nob. How do you deal with guilt?
2. How would your church act toward an ex-convict who wanted to join your congregation? Would he be warmly received? How can you help to make your church a welcoming place to all kinds of people?
3. Read verse 7. Where can you see the same pattern of behaviour today? What does it do to the people who believe in this way? What is their destiny (verse 5)?

Psalm 53

In case you've forgotten

We'd be foolish to try living without God.

All of us need to be reminded of something once in a while. When it is a vital issue the reminder is all the more important. Here we have the message of Psalm 14 repeated for us almost word for word. All that has been changed is the name given to God. In Psalm 14 the word *Yahweh* (the LORD)

175

was used. Here the word is *elohim* (the divine name for God).

The thrust of Psalm 14 is that only a 'fool' would deliberately choose not to believe in God. The message has not changed. To choose to live our lives without reference to God, we have to be foolish by name and foolish by nature (see 1 Samuel 25).

For the comments on the rest of this psalm please see the study of Psalm 14.

Questions

1. Why do we forget spiritual lessons we have learned and need to be reminded about them?
2. What part can the church play in reminding us of the main things God wants us to know? How effectively does your church do this?
3. How important is it to give time to pray that Jewish people might accept Jesus as their Messiah? How can we help them to hear and understand the gospel?

Psalm 54

How could you do this to me?

We need to deal with our feelings of betrayal.

This is another song which was written out of a sense of betrayal. It follows on from the theme of Psalm 52. There David was reflecting upon his betrayal by Doeg (see 1 Samuel 22:22). Knowing Doeg's character as he did, this did not come as any surprise to him. Here, however, he is reeling from the effects of being betrayed by his own people (see 1 Samuel 23:12–29 and 26:1–25). This was so much harder to comprehend. Why would they do this to him? Had he not on many occasions come to their rescue (see 1 Samuel 23:1–29)?

In God alone can we trust

It is always hard to cope when we feel that we have been let down by people who should really support us. David came to the conclusion that in the end the only person who can ultimately be relied upon is God. This is not to say that other people do not really care. He knows that friends often do want to help, but they do not have the strength or the resources to do so.

There is no such deficiency to be found in God. He not only has the desire to help us, he also has the power to do so. His name or character is our guarantee of this; he is the all powerful One (verse 1).

To the God of unlimited resources David comes with a heartfelt request. He feels as if his back is against the wall. Those who should be his allies have become his enemies. This is difficult for the psalmist to take in because they have no apparent reason for such an attack. He can only conclude that these individuals really do not know him or they would not act in this way. Such undeserved hatred is always baffling and demands a considered response.

In order to reassure himself that God is on his side, he makes a personal declaration of faith. He is convinced that God has both the desire and the strength to sustain him at this time (verses 2–4).

He now turns his attention to those who are attacking him. He asks God to make their evil plans backfire on them. If the Lord will answer his prayers his response will be to offer a sacrifice of praise. He will not forget to show gratitude for the help he received in times of trouble (verses 5–7).

Questions

1. How should you deal with a friendship that goes wrong?
2. How should churches cope when members get angry and leave? Share your experiences of situations that have been either mishandled or rightly handled.
3. How should Christians react when suffering persecution for their faith? What guidance does this psalm offer them? Pray for any you know who are in this situation.

Psalm 55

Handling anger and anxiety

Deep emotions can be deeply disturbing!

Emotional turmoil

David is showing all the signs of being in trouble emotionally in this psalm. He appears to be undergoing a great deal of stress or what someone has called 'emotional meltdown'. His feelings are expressed in his words. What is going on inside him is coming to the surface in his conversations. He is using words like 'distraught' (verse 2), 'suffering' (verse 3), 'anger' (verse 3), 'anguish' (verse 4), 'terrors' (verse 4), 'fear' and 'trembling' (verse 5). Here we find David in the middle of a full blown panic attack.

We can see ourselves reflected in this psalm. Many of us have had times of worry and emotional disturbance. Some of us have experienced the terrors of an anxiety attack. None of us are immune from such episodes including the most committed Christians. We should not feel guilty when we become anxious as it is part of life. Indeed, becoming over-anxious or experiencing a panic attack is now very common. It has been estimated that around 10% of the population have intermittent panic attacks. It is knowing what to do with those feelings when they begin to creep up on us that is the secret.

God is listening

David reveals the resources which are available to him. These same resources are available to us when we feel in danger of being overwhelmed by worry. To begin with he turns to the Lord in prayer. He is very bold in his approach. He basically is saying 'don't ignore me now. I'm in trouble Lord'. He tells the Lord exactly how he feels and at the same time expresses his confidence in him. We can do both in prayer (verse 1).

The prayer itself lacks logic, but we need to remember that at this time his feelings were all over the place. He is in deep trouble and has neither the time, nor the energy, to construct a literary masterpiece. This is a cry for help from the heart.

By the time the psalm concludes David will be able to reveal his complete trust in God (verse 22). But first he is going to talk his problem through with the Lord. Talking about our difficulties out loud in the presence of God is often the first step to solving them.

As David begins to tell God about his situation two feelings come to the forefront. He is both anxious and very angry. His mind is confused and he is experiencing some signs of paranoia, feeling that everybody is against him. When we feel this way our fears are confirmed by the fact that people seem to be either always talking about us or constantly ignoring us (verse 3).

Escape from pain

He is also going through a time of acute emotional torture (verse

4). The Hebrew here literally means 'my heart writhes within me'. We might want to render it, 'my stomach is all knotted up'.

All he wants to do is get away (verse 6). He wants to escape from the situation that is causing him so much pain. Some people, when they are undergoing stress, simply want to sleep their lives away. That is their method of avoiding painful circumstances. Others opt for a holiday to get away from it all. In this way they attempt to disengage themselves from their problems. Sadly, some people seek refuge in drugs or too much alcohol. In doing this they are trying to escape into some private world where all their feelings are numbed and they no longer feel pain. The trouble is that we cannot run away from our problems. Escapism is no real answer.

Dealing with pain

David recognizes that the way to deal with his pain is not to hide it but to ask for help to cope with it. He does not have to repress his anxieties, he can express them. He can hand over the whole situation to the Lord, for David has come to believe that in the Lord he has the best listener of all.

We should not think that David has suddenly discovered the benefits of prayer at this crisis time in his life. That would be far from the truth. He has learned to give himself to prayer when all is going right, so that he can continue in prayer when everything is going wrong. He has learned to put his anchor down before the storm breaks. He is well prepared for difficult times because he knows just what to do. Every day he is disciplined about his prayer times. Three times a day he has periods in prayer (verse 17). Three times a day he focuses all his thoughts on God. This enables him to remember in the dark what he has learned in the light. He has always taken potential worries to the Lord in prayer (Philippians 4:6). In this way he has learned how to let God carry his burdens (verse 22).

The psalmist deals with his anxiety by turning to prayer. But how is he to deal with his angry feelings? He does not want to bottle them up. This would be a great mistake, for anger that is repressed often leads to depression. He does not deny his feelings, he simply expresses them in the presence of God. His words may seem hard to some of us (verses 9–11, 15, 22). If so we need to remember that he is asking for judgment to fall on the enemies of God. He wants punishment to take place for the Lord's sake and not for his.

Reading between the lines, there is a reference here to more than the general group of people he called 'his enemies'. It seems that he is angry because he has been hurt by someone who is very close to him (verses 20–21). It has been suggested that David is referring to the time when his son Absalom led a rebellion against him (see 2 Samuel 15). How could a son hurt a father more than turning against him? This was the pain that he had to endure and sometimes he became very angry about it.

The safety valve he had for his anger was prayer. He felt able to tell God exactly how he felt and that was a tremendous help. He was able to speak out loud his feelings of hurt and bewilderment in the presence of his trusted friend (verses 12–14, 20–21). He did not believe that God would be shocked by whatever he had to say.

Sometimes, as Christians, we can hold back our feelings when it comes to speaking to God. We need to remember that God is not so fragile that he will break because of what we might say.

Handing our pain to God

This pilgrimage of open and honest prayer has enabled David to trust God even more. He is now able to encourage others to put their trust in the Lord (verse 22). The word used here, 'cast', literally means 'hurl' or 'throw'. It implies that we should totally hand over to God those things which weigh us down. This does not mean that all the difficulties of our lives will be instantly removed. Often what it does mean is that we have to learn to allow the Lord to carry us as we carry the burden (see 1 Peter 5:7).

The popular poem, 'Footprints', illustrates this perfectly. The anonymous poet depicts himself as complaining to God that in the most difficult times of his life God seemed to leave his side. There was only one set of footprints in the sand. The Lord's explanation is encouraging. He says that the reason there was only one set of footprints, was that in those difficult times he was carrying the poet in his arms.

When we are tempted towards anxiety or anger we need to learn with David to come openly to the Lord and tell him how we feel. We also need to allow him to carry us over the rough patches in life.

Questions

1. Some people handle anxiety and anger by repressing their feelings, others by expressing them inappropriately ('kicking the cat'), and some by trying to escape ('drowning their sorrows'). What do you tend to do? What guidance does this psalm give you?
2. Sometimes churches make anxious or depressed Christians feel guilty or unspiritual. How does your church rate? Are there people who are trained to counsel and support such sufferers? How could your church improve in this respect?
3. Why do you think there is so much stress around us today? What can Christians do, if anything, to help deal with the causes of stress, as well as helping sufferers?

Psalm 56

Out of the frying pan into the fire!

**In times of pressure and danger,
the best place to run is to the Lord.**

 In trying to avoid Saul's evil clutches, David attempted to find refuge in Gath, a Philistine city, the home of his arch enemies and the place where the giant Goliath grew up. There were probably lots of his angry relatives waiting to take revenge on David. So why did he choose to go there? The simple answer is that desperate times sometimes call for desperate measures. When his back was against the wall he felt he had little choice. David had to escape fast, even if this meant going to a dangerous place and pretending to be mad once he got there (1 Samuel 21:10–15).

Here was David in another 'pressure cooker' situation. He had been in them before and God had rescued him. Although he knew that the Lord had always been on his side before, there must have been occasions when his belief in this was severely tested.

When in trouble turn to God

One lesson he had learnt by experiencing difficulties was that, when things go wrong, it is always better to turn to God for help rather than turn away from him and try to solve the problem yourself.

Here he refuses to turn in on himself and become bitter about his circumstances. Instead he reaches out for God and asks him to respond in mercy. He is willing to stay in the difficult place if he is assured that God will be there with him. What he needs to enable him to remain there is an extra supply of God's loving presence. The implication is that if he knows all is right in his relationship with God he can face almost anything (verses 1–2).

When life takes an uncertain turn it is natural to find ourselves overshadowed by dark clouds of fear. David was no different. He honestly admits that his circumstances were making him afraid. But times of fear can often be turned into opportunities for faith. The psalmist brings his fear to the Lord. In the middle of a terrifying time he is learning how to trust in God. It seems that the scary times can be some of our best learning times. Sometimes we can begin to prove that we really do trust God only when we are going through experiences that are testing us to the limit of our endurance (1 Corinthians 10:13).

In the middle of this frightening episode David invites God to be vitally involved in his life. He looks full into his face and then he realizes that, compared to God's power, human threats are insignificant. In the end the worst other people can do to believers is take their life. In doing this they do us the 'favour' of ushering us into the presence of the One we love (verses 3–4).

Even when we are fully trusting in God there are still real problems to be faced. David's enemies continued to plot, scheme and lie, still determined to bring him down. Instead of trying to sort out the situation in his own strength, however, he trusts in the Lord to act on his behalf. Those opposing him may have been treating him as if he was insignificant, but God never did. Even the tears that trickled down David's face were precious to him. Each one of us is worthwhile as far as God is concerned (verses 5–8).

From fear to faith

The psalm shows David moving steadily from fear to faith. He states his belief that, with the Lord on his side, he is unstoppable.

184

There is nothing that anyone can do to him that is worth worrying about.

In the end he finds true freedom. Initially this meant escaping from the Philistines but there is more to it than that. Real freedom comes when we are liberated from things we fear, especially the fear of death (see Hebrews 2:13–16). If our trust in God outweighs our fears then we are free indeed (verses 9–13).

Questions

1. Why is it difficult to admit that we are sometimes afraid? What do we tend to do with our fear? What should we do?
2. What space do we make in our services for 'tears' (verse 8) and confession of our fear and weakness? What are, or would be, the benefits?
3. 'The notion of God is just a crutch for fearful, inadequate people.' What would you respond to someone who said that to you?

Psalm 57

No hiding place?

When we feel vulnerable, we can take 'refuge in the Lord'.

The background to this psalm is yet again David's life on the run (see 1 Samuel 24:1–15). He is being chased from place to place by the relentless Saul. On this occasion he finds temporary shelter inside a cave. While he is in there

Saul himself arrives and David is able to explain that he is not the king's enemy. Indeed, he has had opportunities to kill Saul but because of his loyalty he has not taken them. Even though Saul appears to have been satisfied with his explanation, however, David wants to take no chances. He prefers to be a live outlaw than a dead friend of the king.

We can imagine the conditions inside the caves where he and his band of men often took refuge. They may have been dark and damp but at least they were secure. While thinking about the safety that the cave provides he lifts his mind to consider a security that only the Lord can offer him.

He then expands his thinking to include the world outside the cave. He now uses a word picture of the Lord caring for him in the same tender way as a mother bird would take care of her young (verses 1–2, see also Ruth 2:12; Matthew 23:37).

He sends up a prayer to heaven. He asks the Lord to ensure that his life reaches its full potential. His greatest concern is that he will live long enough to do all that God intends for him. His prayer has hardly left his lips before he receives an answer. An abundant supply of God's love and faithfulness is given to him to enable him to cope with his present circumstances. Such care and protection are too precious to hurry past. Time needs to be given for thanksgiving and praise to the Lord (verses 2–5).

He sees the unfolding events of his life as evidence of God's involvement. The Lord is acting on his behalf to ensure that his enemies' plans rebound on them.

He is able to remain steady in the middle of awful circumstances because of one fact. He is certain that God loves him. Knowing this means that nothing can happen to him which is outside God's agenda for his life. This assurance is not something to keep quiet about. Indeed it is the kind of thing that praise songs are made of. The music which comes from a grateful heart is the sort the whole world wants to hear. It can even reach heaven itself (verses 6–11).

Questions

1. What does it mean to seek refuge in the Lord (see verse 1)? Why is it possible for our hearts to be steadfast (verse 7) even when we are surrounded by disaster?
2. Why does David talk to himself (verse 7)? Think of some situations your church is currently facing. If it could talk to itself, what do you think it should say?
3. What does it mean to praise God among the nations (see verse 9)? How could your church be more effective in spreading the praise of God in other countries, and among ethnic minorities in your locality?

Psalm 58

Corruption in high places

Sometimes we are shocked by the level of corruption among the nations' leaders.

When the leadership of a nation turns corrupt that country is in severe trouble. If politicians gain a reputation for not telling the truth the society which they represent is in danger of falling apart.

Corruption in high places is nothing new. Greed and abuse of power are as old as human history. Even though we know this to be the case, however, it still comes as a shock when we encounter this kind of institutionalized wickedness for ourselves.

In this psalm David is clearly taken aback by the size and scope of political corruption in his day. Those people who should be worthy of trust deserve it least. They are nothing more than snakes in the grass. Like deadly vipers they continue to inject their deadly poison into the heart of society itself (verses 1–3).

Drastic surgery

The situation is so bad that only God can correct it (Isaiah 24:21). The psalmist asks the Lord to take drastic action. These unscrupulous leaders are like a deadly cancer that has to be surgically removed. Only this divine intervention will save the life of the nation.

David's language appears to be extremely harsh, but sometimes a situation becomes so serious that only radical action will work (verses 6–9). The result of this radical surgery will be the removal of corruption. This will give the nation a new lease of life. In response those who live wholesome lives will rejoice.

We might find the language here too graphic for our taste. But we should remember that those whom the psalmist calls the 'wicked' are individuals who have resolutely chosen to disobey God. Their disobedience is not an occasional thing, it is a way of life. They will never acknowledge God's Lordship in their lives. Derek Kidner says that these are the sinners who have followed their principle of self-regard to the bitter end. Sadly their fate is an ominous one.

David believes that when God steps decisively into human history the whole world will take notice. Everybody will know he is One who always tells the truth and does what is right. With the Lord we have a leader always worth following (verses 10–11).

Questions

1. Do you find the language of this psalm too violent? Why do you think God has put passages like this in the Bible?
2. Why do bad and deceitful boasters sometimes arise even in the church? How should the church deal with them?
3. Why is it important for Christians to care about the kind of

leaders our country has? What can we do to ensure, as far as possible, that our leaders govern justly?

Psalm 59

They seek him here, they seek him there!

When there is no let-up to our problems, the strain can start to show.

 To be constantly under scrutiny must be a terribly trying and exhausting experience. David was watched in this way constantly. His home was regularly the object of stake-outs by King Saul's secret police. If they could have had such things back then, we can be sure that his rooms would have been bugged and his phone lines tapped.

Unwanted visitors

The background to this psalm is the time when David came close to being arrested in the middle of the night. Only his wife Michal's timely warning prevented him from being bundled away by the palace police. If this had happened he probably would never have been seen again (see 1 Samuel 19:11–18).

He feels this constant and uninvited observation by Saul very distressing. These daily encounters of a military kind are all becoming too much for him. In this time of tension David does what he always tries to do. He takes the situation to the Lord in prayer. He asks God to step in and deliver him from these people who are always intruding on his life. They need to be stopped. Their only purpose is to do him harm and he knows that he does not deserve such treatment. No mercy should be shown these individuals because they have shown no mercy to him (verses 1–4).

These enemies of his are nothing more than a pack of street dogs. Like wild dogs they live on rubbish and so it is natural that what comes out of their mouths is fit only for the sewer. They may take themselves seriously, but as far as God is concerned they are little more than a bad joke. Their lives should be spared only so they can act as a reminder to everyone that it is God who laughs last. Ultimately they will get what they really deserve. Their punishment will be worldwide news (verse 13).

Those who have constantly pursued David have a very uncertain future. His own future, on the other hand, looks extremely attractive. He believes that the Lord has all the protection and strength he needs. In God he can find a place where he is safe from any prying eyes. This certainty that comes from faith always leads to a song of praise. This praise song focuses on the loving God who is the source of all our strength (verses 5–17).

Questions

1. How do you feel when someone constantly tries to intrude on your life whether from bad or good motives? What is the best way to handle this?
2. What is the difference between 'prayerful interest' and 'interfering'? How can churches and housegroups demonstrate the former and avoid the latter?
3. Can you think of Christians who for whatever reason have to live constantly under unfriendly scrutiny? How should you pray for them?

Psalm 60

Abandoned by the Lord?

**Times of trouble can be an opportunity
for spiritual reassessment.**

 When things go wrong it can be an opportu-
nity to do some serious soul searching. It is not
necessary to believe that all the difficulties
we might encounter are because we have
displeased God. But when problems come our way it is always
wise to pause and take stock. It could be that the Lord wants to use
these troubled times as opportunities to speak to us, his people.

A military failure

David has been reflecting upon a military reversal suffered by
his armies. While he and his men were on a campaign near the
river Euphrates the armed forces of Edom took the opportunity
to attack Judah from the south (see 2 Samuel 8:1–14). This could
simply have been bad planning on his part. But for David it was
much more serious. He saw behind this event a spiritual issue
and implication. For some reason God had chosen to withdraw
his presence from his people. The result was disastrous. Perhaps
the lesson that David and his men needed to learn was that they
have always to rely on the Lord and not themselves.

A prayer for the nation

The psalmist does not allow himself to dwell on the past. He sees this difficulty as a prompting from heaven to seek the Lord in prayer. He asks God to bring healing and restoration to his people. Previously the whole nation has been staggering around like drunkards under the weight of God's judgment. But now they have learned their lesson and it is time for the burden to be lifted and the blessing restored.

David uses military illustrations to describe the re-establishment of the Lord's presence among his people. As a soldier himself he knows that fighting men are given new courage to continue the battle when they see the king's standard is there with them. The monarch's standard or banner, seen on the battle field, signifies that he is involved in the struggle alongside his men. In a similar way those who trust in God are given fresh determination to continue in the fight of faith when they are assured of the Lord's presence (verse 4).

He appeals to God to demonstrate his strength on their behalf. The use of the phrase 'with your right hand' indicates the power of God (verse 5). He believes that his request will be answered because the Lord's motivation to help is his love (verses 1–5).

David's prayer on behalf of himself and his nation is answered. The Lord speaks in a clear and direct way and his proclamation brings words of great comfort. The very fact that he is willing to speak to his people is a sure sign that any fracture in his relationship with them has been healed.

The Lord says that it is he who is in control of the nations. To him they are little more than accessories. The implication here is that if the people of God trusted him more they would not depend on their own strength to deal with these international situations. The Lord has already shown them what happens when they are left to their own devices ... If he does not help them they are hopeless (verses 6–12).

Learning to rely on the Lord's strength is a challenge for every new generation of believers. We all have a tendency to try and go it alone only to discover that without the Lord's presence any project turns into a disaster. A wise Christian once said that, 'When I try in my own strength I fail, but when I trust in his strength he succeeds.'

Questions

1. C. S. Lewis said that pain is God's megaphone to rouse a deaf world. How has God used painful experiences in order to speak to you?
2. What are the things churches are sometimes tempted to trust in, other than the Lord? How can we guard against the wrong kind of confidence?
3. Who or what are the 'enemies' Christians battle against today? How can we support one another in the fight?

Psalm 61

The rock that is higher than I

When we long for security we can find it in the 'rock-like' reliability of God.

It is never a pleasant experience to feel lonely, isolated or vulnerable. At times like these we crave for security and we want to be reassured that somebody, some-where cares about us.

Separated from the one I love

David wrote this psalm when he was feeling that everybody was standing at a distance from him. Even the Lord seemed to be a long way away. His prayers seemed to be of the 'long distance' variety. The very effort of trying to keep in contact with the Lord was exhausting him.

Yet even in this period of sensing a distance between himself and the One he loved, David was sure of one thing. Whatever problem he was facing God could be trusted to deal with it. Despite his feelings the psalmist never lost confidence in the fact that there was somebody who was big enough to take care of any eventuality.

He speaks of God as being like a huge rock. This is a picturesque way of describing the Lord's power and protection. It also conveys his 'rock solid' reliability (verses 1–2).

God is always there

In this psalm the writer reviews his personal history. He concludes that God has always taken care of him. For instance, when his enemies had been hard on his tail he was able to run to the Lord and find protection. He had proved that trusting in God was better than putting his faith in the strongest man-made fortress.

The description of his relationship with the Lord now takes on a different complexion. Instead of talking in military terms about the Lord's protection, he now pictures the warm hospitality offered by a welcoming friend. He wants to live as God's house guest for ever (see Psalm 23:6). He wants to be as close to him as possible. The psalmist believes that he will find loving care and protection if he stays close to the Lord. In the same way as a mother bird protects her young under her wing at the first sign of danger, so the Lord will wrap his protective love around his servant (verse 4).

For the psalmist his relationship with God is the most important thing in his life. He takes his commitments to the

Lord very seriously indeed. He believes that God always honours those who show due respect to his name (verses 3–5).

Living every day for the Lord

The psalm concludes with a prayer. It is David's request to God to grant him a long life. The gift of extended life expectancy will not be wasted. He will make every effort to live each day in close fellowship with the Lord. For he wants to know not only the intimacy of God's presence but also the security of his protection. The guarantee that this will take place is the fact that God is always faithful.

As the psalmist considers the path ahead he believes his time will be taken up with two special activities. He will practise obedience to the Lord and participate in praise and worship.

This stress on fulfilling our commitments to the Lord is very important (verse 8). It is a theme that other song writers have picked up throughout the history of the church. Hundreds of years later another song was written which makes the same point. The chorus of this song says:

> Trust and obey
> For there's no other way
> To be happy in Jesus
> But to trust and obey.

Questions

1. What does the term 'rock' suggest you to about the character of God? How does this encourage you as you face any current difficulties?
2. What kind of security can the church offer people in an insecure world? Why aren't more people attracted to it?
3. David wants to live to a ripe old age. How do we regard the elderly? What contributions can they make to our fellowships?

Psalm 62

Real rest ... real peace

The only way to achieve lasting peace is to place our trust in God.

We can only truly rest when our hearts and minds are at peace. Most of us know what it's like to have something on our minds when we go to bed. Even if we are able to get some sleep, we wake the next morning as exhausted as we were the night before. Our bodies may have been resting but our minds were still racing.

God's peace

St Augustine said 'our hearts are restless till they find their rest in You.' We can only find real peace when we make our peace with God. It seems that David was discovering the truth of this. He testifies to the fact that the only true rest he has found in his life is 'resting in the Lord'. This does not mean retreating from the world in order to find some peace and quiet. It is the peace that can be known in the middle of hectic activity. This comes by daily turning over to the Lord all that we are doing.

Instead of carrying the weight of the world around on his shoulders, David has learned to give the burden to the Lord. In this way he can cope. When he trusts in the Lord he feels secure. He rests in the fact that God is strong enough to take care of him. Society might be shaking itself to pieces but the believer is able to stay together (verses 1–2).

In his own strength David is as easy to knock down as a badly built wall. But with the Lord's resources he can stand up to anyone and anything. The secret of his inner strength is that he has learned to tap into God's unlimited supply of power. In this way he can be at peace when everything around him is chaotic. For the psalmist there is no need to fear as he can rest in the Lord (verses 3–7).

This sense of inner well being leads David to encourage others to follow his example. We can all discover for ourselves that God can be trusted with every aspect of our lives. Even when things go wrong there is no need to panic. We have the provision of prayer. Simply knowing that God is aware of what is going on in our lives is a great comfort. He invites his listeners to pour out to the Lord all their problems. They are to hold back nothing at all. In this way they are demonstrating that they really do trust the Lord to take care of their lives. Learning to trust the Lord in everything is vital to the life of faith (verse 8).

No peace without trust in God

David now contrasts those who place their trust in God and those who rely on their own resources. It makes no difference whether someone is born into a rich family or poor one. Nor is the source of the wealth a decisive factor. What really counts is whether they trust in the Lord or not. This is the real division in society. Even those who are rich beyond anyone's wildest dreams he counsels to trust in God rather than in gold (verses 9–10).

Any parent knows that sometimes saying a thing once is not sufficient. The psalmist repeats himself to ensure that everyone is getting his message. He wants everyone to know that God is the only truly dependable person in the universe. He is reliable because he has the strength to achieve all that he intends to. He is approachable because his love ensures he has our best interests at heart. When we really begin to understand this we can have true rest and perfect peace (verses 11–12).

Questions

1. Paul encourages his readers to love God and be content with what he provides (see 1 Timothy 6:6). Why is it so hard to be content? How can we learn to be more content?
2. Given that rich and poor are equally a 'breath' (verse 9) and that riches should not be important to us (verse 10), why are churches often such middle-class places? How can we make them fellowships where everybody will feel at home?
3. Think about the inequality of rich and poor nations. Is there a sense in which rich nations are stealing and extorting from the poor (verse 10)? What can we do to encourage greater equality?

Psalm 63

I long for you Lord

Nothing but meeting with the Lord can really satisfy us.

Physical experiences can sometimes reflect how we feel spiritually. There is no doubt that when he wrote this psalm David was reflecting back on a time when he was physically thirsty. The title tells us that he had experienced a period of wandering in the desert of Judah. This may refer to the time when he was forced out of Jerusalem by the rebellion led by his son Absalom (see 2 Samuel 15:23). This trek through the wilderness under the hot desert sun must have been very tortuous indeed. David probably experienced acute thirst and was desperate for something to drink.

Spiritual thirst

In this psalm David explores what it means to be spiritually thirsty. He obviously had been through times when he was so desperate for God that it hurt. People travelling through a hot and arid land need water to quench their thirst. Only a cool refreshing drink will meet their real need. Likewise, when we become thirsty for God's presence in our lives only his refreshing touch will do.

The psalmist is certainly not playing at religion. He views his relationship with the Lord as a matter of life and death. A person deprived of water in a hot climate will soon dehydrate and die. In the spiritual realm it is equally dangerous to become dehydrated. Recognizing this, the psalmist is passionate about meeting the Lord. Nothing short of a direct encounter with him will do. Only God can really quench his thirst (verse 1).

He recalls times when he has met with God in a special way. For him it was a powerful and glorious experience. This had given him a taste of what things could be like. Now he wants that vital form of relationship with the Lord more than anything else in the world.

Receiving from and giving to God

David is obviously passionate about prayer. But he is equally positive when it comes to praise. In prayer he receives from the Lord, and in praise he returns something to the Lord. He fully intends to give his whole life to the worship of God. This kind of praise cannot be limited to words alone. He wants to offer everything to the Lord. He believes that it is a case of all or nothing when it comes to worship (see Romans 12:1–3).

As was the custom he lifts up his hands to heaven when he is praying and praising. This signifies two things: a willingness to give everything to the Lord, and a willingness to receive whatever the Lord wants to give to us (verses 2–5).

When other people are asleep David is occupying his time with thoughts of God. The quietness of the night allows him time to meditate on all the blessings that God has brought into his life. Sometimes prayer and praise has to be a twenty-four-hour-a-day activity.

Even in this time when he is seeking to be close to the Lord his enemies are not far from his mind. This is probably the way it must always be, for the devil is always more active when we get serious about our faith. In the end, however, all those who oppose God and his people will meet an awful fate.

The psalmist refuses to be deflected from his aim of meeting with the Lord. Those who trouble him are defeating their own purposes. For when they bring pressure to bear upon him they only drive him back to prayer. He then has yet another opportunity to meet with the only one who can truly satisfy his soul (verses 6–11).

Questions

1. How does your determination to meet with God compare with David's? Why are we sometimes not very thirsty for God?
2. To David, worship in the sanctuary had been an oasis in a desert (verses 1–2). How can we make sure that our church is an oasis for thirsty people, and not 'dry and weary'?
3. Do Christians really demonstrate to the world that our relationship with God is more important than life itself? If not, why not?

Psalm 64

God will take care of them

God can be trusted to 'take care of' those who oppose us.

 This psalm picks up where the previous one left off. These enemies of David, who come so often in the Psalms, seem to be up to their evil activities yet again. But perhaps they have overreached themselves where David is concerned. It seems that those who try to attack succeed in only one thing. They drive him to God in prayer. Viewed in this light anyone who tries to make our lives uncomfortable is really doing us a favour. In reality they will simply turn us into men and women of prayer.

The psalm begins with David complaining to God about those who wish to do him harm. He asks the Lord to keep him safe during this testing time. In his prayer he tells him all about the various plots and schemes that his enemies are employing. These are the kind of individuals who tend to congratulate themselves when they have devised a particularly nasty trap for someone. They are not nice people to know (verses 1–6).

God's enemies

What David is able to discern through prayer is the fate of his enemies and it does not make for pleasant reading. In the end

201

they will all run right into his secret weapon. God himself will fight against them. This is based upon the principle that an enemy of a child of God is, in reality, an enemy of God himself. They will face his awful judgment. The way this will be worked out is quite frightening. All their plans will boomerang back on themselves. The things they intend to hurt David with will in the end hurt them. This is how God deals with those who want to oppose him and his people.

It is always amazing how prayer can turn negatives into positives. Here David has had his enemies attacking him and yet some good comes of it. If he had never experienced opposition he would never have seen God at work dealing with his opponents. Furthermore, if there had been no need of the Lord's intervention there would be no opportunity to testify to his mighty acts. So a lot of good has come out of a very bad situation. This often seems to be the way the Lord chooses to work (verses 7–9).

The psalm concludes with an invitation for everybody who loves God and lives an upright life to praise him (verse 10).

Questions

1. What can we learn from this psalm about a 'sharp tongue'? How have you felt when someone has attacked you with the tongue? Have you been guilty of this yourself? How should we use our tongues (verses 9–10)?
2. Read verse 6. Can you think of examples of this kind of 'politicking' even in the church? If we have strong views about the direction our church should take, how should we go about gaining acceptance for them?
3. How should Christians deal with the plotting and the planning, the bullying and the smear tactics, that sometimes occur in our workplace when people are seeking their own advancement?

Psalm 65

We come to worship

When we think of what God has done for us we sing with thanksgiving.

Our modern word 'worship' comes from an Anglo Saxon word 'weorthscipe'. This meant 'to give someone their worth ship'. This psalm begins by stating that God really is worth praising! The Lord is not only worthy of our praise, he is also worthy of our respect. When we really respect people we will always try to keep our promises to them.

Confidence in prayer

David tells us that he is confident that the Lord always hears his prayers. In heaven the phone is never left off the hook where prayer is concerned. It is particularly important that we have this free access to God when we are feeling defeated by our own sinfulness. When things have gone seriously wrong in our lives it's good to know that we can tell the Lord all about it.

We do not know exactly what has happened to David. Whatever it was has left him feeling tremendously guilty. Indeed he feels that he is almost drowning in a sea of guilt. The good news is that the Lord will not only listen to his confession, he will also offer him cleansing. The psalmist can leave this time of prayer assured that his sins are forgiven. God himself is willing to pay the price for this freedom from a guilty conscience (see Mark 10:45).

He counts it a privilege to have been chosen by God to live for him. Living in such intimacy with the Lord is the most satisfying relationship a person can know (verses 1–4). David now widens the scope of this vision. Instead of concentrating on his own circumstances, he takes into account the whole population of the world. For them, God is their only hope. But if he is able to take care of all the planet's needs he is surely able to look after the people who live on it. When this concept is understood the result is joy. Those who know that they are the Lord's join with all nature in loud and boisterous praise. He is certainly worth it (verses 5–13).

Questions

1. How can we give God his 'worth ship' every day, both in our prayer times and in the ordinary activities of life?
2. Verse 4 speaks of 'the good things of your [God's] house'. What are the 'good things of your church'?
3. What do verses 9–13 tell us about God's care for the natural world he created? How does this speak to us about our own care for the environment?

Psalm 66

No noise ... no life

Sometimes our praise makes us shout for joy.

The Cornish tin miner Billy Bray always found it extremely difficult to remain silent in church. He could often be heard to shout 'Amen' or 'Hallelujah' during the service. This really bothered some members of the congregation. One of the richer members took it upon himself to offer Billy an incentive to keep quiet. He promised him a new shirt if he would keep silent throughout one entire Sunday service. A new shirt was a very tempting prospect to Billy who was very poor indeed. So he promised to try to do as the man had asked.

The particular Sunday arrived and the service was in progress. True to his word Billy was keeping quiet, though with some difficulty. But as the preacher began to speak of the love of God Billy became more and more agitated. In the end he could stand it no more. He rose to his feet and shouted at the top of his lungs, 'shirt or no shirt hallelujah'.

Silence isn't always golden

There are times when it is right to be silent in church. There are other times when the only thing we can do is praise God with a loud voice. This anonymous psalm encourages us to 'shout' and 'sing' to the glory of God. His love is too precious to keep quiet about. The joy that the Spirit brings needs an outlet. We must allow praise to flow out from the people of God. Wherever there is life there will be noise.

The psalmist is not satisfied with limiting the shouts of praise to a local congregation. He wants the whole earth to take part. Everybody should join in the song which praises the Lord for his mighty power and strength. In the presence of such awesome power the enemies of God can only cower like frightened puppies. He is a God to be feared!

The only position we can adopt when meeting with the living Lord is flat on our face. The word 'bow' literally means 'to prostrate oneself'. Here then the psalmist gives us an incredible picture. In the presence of God's greatness the whole world can do nothing but fall flat on the floor. The novelist Fyodor Dostoevsky was correct when he wrote, 'The one essential condition of human existence is that man should always be able to bow down to something infinitely great'. To remain standing in these circumstances would be the worst form of pride and ignorance. Someone has said, 'when you really meet face to face with God the only safe place to be is on your knees' (verses 1–4).

Come and see what God has done

The psalmist's sanctified imagination allows him to see the population of the world responding to the divine invitation. They are invited to come and view God's marvellous achievements: how he stepped into history in order to save his people, and how he used his miraculous power to part the Red Sea so that they might escape from the Egyptian army. Such powerful interventions by God deserve the most positive response (verses 5–7).

The psalm continues with this theme of praise. The writer

refers back to periods in Israel's history when things were really tough. Many of these difficulties were brought about by the people's own rebellion against God. Yet despite this the Lord always came through for them. He did not simply save them, he also brought them into a time of rich blessing (verses 8–12).

At this point the psalmist speaks of his own personal commitment to the Lord. He is determined to live a life that is characterized by costly worship and wholehearted obedience. He wants everyone to recognize that sin has no place in the life of the believer. For where sin is deliberately held on to the lines of communication to heaven are cut. He is confident that there is nothing that he is aware of which might block the pathway of prayer (verses 13–20).

The psalm which began with a shout of confident praise ends with a sigh of confidence in prayer.

Questions

1. How does God 'refine' his people (see verses 10–12)? How should we respond to this refining?
2. Why do we find both silence and noise disturbing in our worship services? Is it good to encourage full hearted and sometimes very noisy worship in our churches? Why or why not?
3. When we share the gospel with others, how important is it that we should be able to tell them what God has done for us personally? What could you share with them from your own experience of God?

Psalm 67

Shine on me

We long that everyone in the world will experience God's love.

The first line of this psalm is often used as a concluding prayer in church services. It echoes the words which Moses gave to the priest Aaron as a priestly blessing for the people (see Numbers 6:23–26).

God's blessing

This psalm reads so positively. It is concerned with ensuring that God's blessing reaches out to the whole world. Like ripples on a pond spreading out to the furthest bank, the psalmist wants the Lord's special favour to spread out across the whole world.

He asks that God's blessing might begin with his people, and that they might have an honest, open relationship with the Lord. He longs that they might experience the warmth of the smile of God upon their lives (verse 1).

The psalmist is not wanting to keep all the blessing to himself and his immediate circle of friends, however. He wants the joy he has discovered in knowing the Lord to be shared by everyone. As in the case of Abraham, the blessing might begin with an individual but it was always the Lord's intention to bless the whole world (verse 2, see also Genesis 12:1–3; Acts 1:8).

The nations of the world which do experience the salvation of the Lord will have many reasons to praise him. They will want to thank him for his acts of righteousness on their behalf. He will not leave them to stumble blind through life. He constantly offers wise guidance. This will contribute to the groundswell of worldwide praise to the Lord.

This theme of global praise is now developed further. The result of this praiseful attitude to God will be a rich harvest of blessing. As other members of the world's population observe this they will be in awe of such a great God (verses 5–7).

Questions

1. We often ask God to 'bless' us, but what, according to this psalm, does God's blessing result in? (Look especially at verses 1, 2, 6 and 7.) How does this compare with the way we often use the Word?
2. What is your church doing to help make salvation known among all nations (verse 2)? How can we catch the psalmist's enthusiasm for this?
3. How can God be said to rule the peoples justly and guide the nations, given that they do not acknowledge him in any meaningful sense?

Psalm 68

Where the real power lies

Our God is both a victorious General and a loving Father.

In this psalm David wants everybody to know that when it comes to power, God has no real competitors. In a striking use of picture language he compares the enemies  of the Lord to smoke which is so easily blown away by the wind. He uses a second picture to compare those who deliberately disobey God (the wicked) to wax which melts away before the heat of a flame. The implication here is that no-one can stand up before the Lord's superior strength (verses 1–2).

Throughout the psalms there is always a contrast between those who stand against the Lord and those who stand with him. God's enemies have nothing positive to look forward to. His friends, on the other hand, have every reason to rejoice about the future.

Reasons for joy

David now lists all the reasons why God's people should be joyful and offer him praise. To begin with he is the great defender of the defenceless. He takes care of those who cannot take care of themselves. The psalmist illustrates this by giving examples of those who, in his society, were most vulnerable. These included orphans and widows who had no social service schemes to fall back on in those days. If members of their own family could not take care of them they were forced to beg or to starve.

There were many lonely people in David's day, even when the family structure was so much stronger than it is now. Today there are millions of people around the world who feel that no-one cares whether they live or die. From this psalm it appears that the Lord has a particular interest in these people. He offers them a chance to join his extended family.

There is an obvious application here for our own churches and Christian groups. As families continue to break up and society continues to fragment Christians can play a vital role. The churches can become a 'family' for all those who are inwardly dying from lack of love. To have lonely people in an area where Christians live is a rebuke to our care for the community.

The Lord does not only care for the lonely, he also cares for those who have been wrongly imprisoned. We may infer from this that the Lord wants not just literal prisoners but all those who feel themselves trapped by their circumstances to find liberty (Isaiah 61:1, 2; Luke 4:16–19). Wherever people find release from oppression the result is usually joy expressed in song (verses 3–6).

The psalmist continues listing the various reasons why the Lord's people should rejoice. He not only takes care of their needs in the present, but he also offers to go ahead of them to ensure a secure future. Nothing can stand in his way. This means that nothing can stop those who are with him. Any threats from his enemies are futile. The only option for these would-be opponents is to hoist the white flag of surrender (verses 7–18).

Part of the blessing of being a believer is having the knowledge that there is no burden we have to carry by ourselves alone. The psalmist implies here that even the heavy weight of worrying about death can be lifted by the Lord (verses 19–20).

A glorious homecoming

In the last section of the psalm David pictures God as a great general returning home from a famous battle victory. It may be that he was drawing on his own experience of a victory parade which celebrated the recapture of the Ark (see 2 Samuel 6:1–15). In a similar way, the Lord's procession includes singers and musicians. Instrumental music and song were often a part of the victory celebrations (Exodus 15:19–21; 1 Samuel 18:6). Representatives of some of the families of Israel are there too, joining in this marvellous spectacle.

This is a time to rejoice in God's power. He is able to deal with anything the opposition might like to throw at him. The psalmist is convinced that if we are on the Lord's side we are bound to be on the winning team (verses 28–31).

This psalm gives us so many reasons to praise God. It concludes with an invitation to all the earth's inhabitants to join together to worship the Lord (verses 32–35).

Questions

1. How willing would you be to take a homeless person into your home? What difficulties might there be? What other things could you do to befriend a lonely person?
2. What steps can your church take to try and ensure that there are no lonely people in your neighbourhood? How can the church be a real family to them?
3. There are many forms of imprisonment. What kinds can you think of? What can Christians do to help people find real freedom? What will this involve?

Psalm 69

People pressure

We can feel under real pressure because of other people's unkindness.

 The previous psalm concluded on a high note of praise. This song begins lower down the scale, on a note of panic. If David was on the mountain top before, now he is languishing around in the deepest and darkest valley.

Why he felt like this is uncertain. But the problem he is facing is obviously very serious indeed. He feels as if he is being swamped by his circumstances. Like a drowning man he is sinking below the waves in danger of never surfacing again.

When prayer doesn't seem to work

He informs us that he has already tried the 'prayer route' in order to deal with the problem. All he has to show for his long hours of intercession is fatigue and a very sore throat! He has been searching for some sight of God in all this, but all he has got for his trouble is spiritual eyestrain.

This is a common complaint that he voices in the psalm. He believes that he is in deep trouble and in need of God's help. But at a time when he needs him most the Lord seems to help least!

God seems to have gone missing and he is left alone to face the indignity of false accusations (verses 1–3).

He asks the question that so many of us have asked when things go wrong. Why is this happening to me? He begins to investigate whether there is some sin which he has not dealt with. Perhaps this has brought about this difficulty? David concludes that he does not believe 'sin' to be the real problem here. After all, he has made a practice of allowing the Lord to have free access to every area of his life. He has not tried to hide anything from him (verses 4–5).

The psalmist now begins to list all the things that are going wrong in his life. His friends and family alike are constantly teasing him because of his religious enthusiasm. The local bully boys divide their time equally between drinking bouts and targeting him for profanity and abuse. It all seems so unfair (verses 6–12). Remarkably he does not give up. Instead he persists in prayer.

In his prayers the psalmist asks the Lord to lend him a hand. He wants to be pulled up out of the swamp in which he finds himself. Only God has the power to rescue him. If the Lord would come to his aid he is sure that all will be well (verses 13–18).

The prayer continues by reminding God that he knows all the facts about the situation. He is the only One to whom David could possibly turn. The others to whom he had turned for help had all let him down. This was difficult to accept and even more difficult to forgive (verses 19–28).

Persistent prayer works

There is little doubt that he is in utter turmoil because of what is happening to him. All he can do is ask for the Lord's gracious help. As he prays he begins to look in faith toward the future. He believes that God will, at some stage, intervene on his behalf (verse 33). When this happens he will not forget to say thank you. He will express his gratitude to the Lord in praise and worship.

This saving act of God will be a powerful testimony to others. Those who are suffering poverty will be able to see that there really is someone who cares about them (verses 29–33).

The psalm concludes with David inviting all creation to praise the Lord. He also looks forward to the time when all those who love God will be able to live together as one family. What a homecoming that will be (verses 34–36).

Questions

1. Why does David feel that others of God's people might be 'disgraced' because of him (verse 6)? Have you ever felt like that?
2. Why don't most Christians fast any more? What place might there be for fasting today?
3. David looked for sympathy and comfort in his distress, but found only scorn (verse 20). Do we tend to despise people who are not coping? What would giving them real comfort involve?

Psalm 70

I want patience ... and I want it now!

Sometimes we find it difficult to 'wait for the Lord'.

We are told that patience is a virtue. The sad truth is that this is a quality that most of us just do not have. If we are really honest we are the kind of individuals who say, 'Lord give me patience...and give it to me now'!

None of us knows how patient we are until our patience is put to the test. One such test is when we have asked the Lord for something and he seems to be keeping us waiting. This can be a difficult test to pass!

No quick answers

It appears that David has asked the Lord to do something in prayer and the answer was not quick in coming. He is clearly impatient for the Lord to act. As far as he is concerned his situation is critical and needs some divine action sooner rather than later (verse 1).

The reason for his impatience is that his enemies were up to their old tricks with him again. These were individuals who constantly plotted against him. They even went so far as to plan to murder him. In light of this he asks God to step in and stop their plans by throwing them into confusion. The psalmist wants this to be done in a very public way. It is important for him that everyone recognizes that what his enemies are doing is a disgrace. In contrast to this he wants all of society to know that honouring the Lord is the best choice in life. A person who makes this wise choice will have a life characterized by joy and praise (verses 2–5).

If we can learn to wait patiently for the Lord to act we will have so much more peace. It certainly is not easy but it will be worth it in the end.

Questions

1. Why is it so hard to wait for God to act? What do we tend to do rather than allowing God to act in his own way and in his own time?
2. One setting in which we often get impatient for God to act is in the local church. What are some of the results of this?
3. Why doesn't God always do immediately things that seem

to us to be very good? What do we learn in the waiting period?

Psalm 71

When I get older losing my hair

─────────

We don't like thinking about growing old.

─────────

There are lots of amusing sayings about the topic of ageing. Here are some. You know that you are growing old when: 'Everything hurts, and what does not hurt does not work', or when 'You get winded playing chess'.

Or perhaps you have heard growing old described as reaching the 'metallic age'. That is when you get silver in your hair, gold in your teeth and lead in your feet.

Now these may appear to be quite humorous. But to some people the prospect of growing old is horrific. The real fear of reaching old age is being unwanted and unloved. This unnamed psalm explores the subject of ageing with great openness and honesty.

The writer begins by reminding the Lord that he has placed his whole trust in him. In the light of this he asks that he will never have to be ashamed of being a believer. The implication here is that there is some doubt in his mind that God will take care of him in the future. If the Lord were to let him down it would be very bad publicity indeed for all concerned.

Abandoned in old age?

The absolute honesty found here is to be applauded. The psalmist is frightened by the ageing process, he does have nagging doubts about the future. He has even worried that when he reaches old age he might be abandoned by everyone, including God. With these thoughts in mind he speaks plainly to the Lord. If God did not continue to care for him it would be just the opportunity his enemies needed to ridicule his faith and his Lord (verses 1–14).

He reasons with himself about the issue. He tells himself that it is impossible for God to abandon a person who had always placed his trust in him. As he has no intention of abandoning the Lord in the future, surely the Lord would not desert him? Yet, despite his closely argued thoughts, doubts still remain. To deal with these fears he turns again to the Lord in prayer. He asks for God to stay close to him in his later years.

He does not only want peace of mind about the future. He wants to be assured of undiminishing supplies of spiritual power in order that he might complete his work of preaching. He is concerned about the next generation's need to know about the Lord. Given the power to do so he will ensure that they do (verses 15–18).

God cares for old and young

The writer comforts himself about the future by reflecting on the fact that God always does what's right. He is the One who is in ultimate control of the past, the present, and the future. The psalmist has proved him in the past, he is trusting in him in the present, surely he can rely on him in the future (verses 17–18).

It seems that this debate with himself has worked. The tremors of doubt appear to have passed. The psalm now concludes, not with a sense of panic about what the future holds, but with praise to God for his faithfulness. The writer has come to the place where he trusts his life to the One who offers unchanging love from the cradle to beyond the grave (verses 19–24).

Growing stronger as the years pass

This psalm should help to remind us that God is no respecter of age. He can use us at any time in our lives. John Wesley at eighty-five years old was not worn out by his extensive activities. (He had travelled 250,000 miles on horseback, preached 40,000 sermons, written 400 books and learnt to speak ten languages). Wesley attributed his youthful activity to four things.

1. Exercise and a change of air.
2. Never having lost a night's sleep on land or sea.
3. Rising at 4 a.m. every morning.
4. Preaching at 5 a.m. each morning for fifty years.

When he had reached eighty-six years of age, Wesley was annoyed that he could not write for more than fifteen hours a day. At eighty-seven he was ashamed that he could not preach more than twice a day. He even confessed to having a growing urge to stay in bed after 5.30 in the morning!

Growing older is a daunting prospect for all of us. But if we, like the psalmist, learn to go regularly to God with our needs and concerns we will discover he is rock-like and reliable even when we are becoming physically weaker and more feeble (verse 3). If we place our trust in him we can face our advancing years with faith not fear, with praise not panic (verses 14 and 23)!

Questions

1. Why do we fear growing old? Older people in the group: How does your experience of being old compare with what you expected?
2. Churches are often very youth-oriented, yet the number of elderly people in society is growing. How can your church reach out to them, use their experience and offer practical help if needed?
3. Most cultures have honoured their old people and valued

their wisdom. What kind of deal do old people get in our society? Where improvement is needed, how can we work for change?

God uses older people

God can and often does use older people to do mighty works for him. All that is required of them is that they retain a passion of the Lord and his work. According to Acts 7:20–51 Moses was in his eighties before he took on the leadership of the people of Israel. Caleb at eighty-five wanted to take on the most arduous tasks for the Lord (see Joshua 14:6–15). The Apostle John was probably in his nineties when he was enduring persecution and writing the book of Revelation (Revelation 1). It appears to be our attitude and not our age which really affects our service for God.

Psalm 72

God save the King

This psalm points us forward to the perfect King, Jesus.

This is the last psalm in this part of the collection. It is written by David's son, Solomon and is a prayer in which he asks for God's help in order to rule well.

A just ruler

Solomon knows that a godly king will be one who deals with his subjects in a way in which the Lord would approve. He will be the kind of ruler who does the right thing in the right way. A godly king will ensure that those who are least able to take care of themselves receive his full protection and help. It goes without saying that a kingdom governed by such a monarch will experience blessing and prosperity (verses 1–4).

The king who honours God will enjoy a long and fruitful life. His reign will not end with his death because he will have sons to carry on his line (verses 5–7). This will all be a part of God's blessing on him.

When this king speaks the whole earth will listen. All the other national leaders will beat a path to his door. They will all become his servants and do his will.

Yet despite having all this power, privilege and prestige this king will have time for his poorest subjects. He will not only care for those who are 'up and in', he will also care for those who are 'down and out'. He will make sure that he meets regularly with the needy. Programmes to care for disadvantaged will be put in place. Each individual is worthwhile as far as he is concerned (verses 5–14).

A long reign

With such a wonderful description of this ruler it is no wonder that his subjects never want his reign to come to an end. His people are constantly praying for his welfare and well-being. They know that as long as he is in control all the nations of the world will be blessed (verses 15–17).

The heavenly King

The psalm ends by reminding us that even the best human king is subject to a more mighty Monarch. In the end it is God who should receive all the praise. It was the Lord, after all, who gave this great king all the strength, wisdom and power he needed to reign (verses 18–19).

Like so many of the psalms these words take us beyond thinking about an earthly king to reflect upon the greater glory of a king who was to come. His name is King Jesus.

The postscript at the end of the psalm informs us that this concludes David's contribution for the time being. We will encounter more of his prayers later in the psalm collection.

Questions

1. What does this psalm tell us about King Jesus? What is it like for you to be his subject?
2. If the church really lived under the authority of its King, what kind of community would it be, according to this psalm?
3. If Jesus is our model, how should we exercise the authority that belongs to us as parents, teachers, church leaders, or in other roles at work or in society that involve leading and supervising others?

Further reading

John Goldingay, *Songs from a Strong Land* (Psalms 42–51) (IVP, 1978).

G. A. F. Knight, *The Daily Study Bible (Old Testament)*, *Psalms* Volumes I and II (St Andrew's Press, 1983).

Derek Kidner, Volume I, *Psalms 1–77*, Volume II, *Psalms 78–150* (IVP, 1973).

C. S. Lewis, *Reflections on the Psalms* (Fontana/Collins, 1961).

Tremper Longman II, *How to read the Psalms* (IVP, 1988).

C. H. Spurgeon, *The Treasury of David*, Volumes 1–7 (Evangelical Press, 1977).

John Stott, *Favourite Psalms* (Candle Books, 1994).